Kathryn
Happy birthday 2002.
Love Mum & Dad. X

# fragrant
# herb
# garden

# fragrant herb garden

## lesley bremness

**photography by clay perry**

Quadrille

To Araminta Whitley, for inspired guidance.

Publishing Director: **Anne Furniss**

Project Editor: **Nicki Marshall**

Art Editor: **Rachel Gibson**

Production: **Vincent Smith, Julie Hadingham**

First published in 2000 by Quadrille Publishing Ltd,
Alhambra House, 27–31 Charing Cross Road, London WC2H 0LS

Based on material originally published in *Crabtree & Evelyn Fragrant Herbal*.

Cataloguing in Publication Data: a catalogue record for this book is available
from the British Library.

ISBN 1 902757 33 5

Printed in Hong Kong

*Page 1: The refreshing brightness of double-flowered Chamomile, Calendula
and Crisp Leaf Tansy.*

*Page 2: The encompassing delight of aromatic herbs.*

*Page 4: A potager bed of Lavender and Parsley.*

# contents

# INTRODUCTION

*The more we take time to know the versatile range of plants we call herbs, the more life-enhancing properties they reveal. The new aspects explored in this book are based on the ability of fragrant herbs to lift our spirits. From earliest times sweet perfumes have delighted the mind and body of human beings but now we can choose specific fragrances to enhance a chosen mood. Recent scientific experiments confirm that scents such as Mint stimulate the limbic system, the part of the brain concerned with basic emotions and instinctive actions, while others like Sweet Pea relax it. We can fine-tune this information with personal experience and choose the herbs that work best for us.*

*The refined pleasures of fragrant plants have been glorified throughout history. In Egyptian temple gardens aromatic plants were grown for use in sacred rituals. Cleopatra acquired an incense tree plantation worth a small kingdom to ensure a regular supply of resinous gums. Persian poems and paintings allude to the atmosphere of garden perfumes with seats positioned to catch the drift of flowers on the breeze. In Chinese gardens the anticipation of scented pleasure was heightened with calligraphy announcing 'The Pavilion of Fragrant Clouds' or 'Moonlight in the Pines'.*

*Fragrance has a subtle yet powerful effect on our moods because smell was the first of our senses to evolve, and this is why scent can so instantly evoke a memory. As it was once our main defensive tool it was connected to survival instincts, such as hunger, thirst, sex and danger. We now have our mammalian brain overlaying the limbic system with 'human' qualities, but the links are still there. The perfume industry, supermarkets and car showrooms rely on these ancient connections, with 'smart building' systems now designed to inject chosen scents into air conditioning to revitalize staff or aid concentration.*

*We too can use positive relaxing scent messages to counter the agitated signals produced by stress. The purest and most effective scents are those from growing plants because their atomic, magnetic and chemical properties resonate most closely with the human system. Flowers give their perfume freely to attract pollinators, but leaves need to be pressed to release their scent. Those fortunate enough to have a garden, conservatory or window space have a glorious opportunity to create a fragrant nurturing area. As summer sun, light rain or a brushing hand release several plant fragrances they combine to create the earth's most perfect but elusive perfume – fragrant fresh air.*

# CULTIVATING THE SENSES

*Taking an appreciative look at how all our senses can be charmed by scented herbs not only increases our general gardening pleasure but also heightens our enjoyment of their fragrance. Selecting aromatic species of herbs for their mood-enhancing qualities we can choose particular varieties for their colour and texture to give extra pleasure to our other senses. Widening our considerations to include the garden at night, starlight offers a different visual beauty while making us more aware of the sounds of the night and sharpening our sensitivity to evening perfumes such as Honeysuckle, Evening Primrose and Jasmine. Planted and tended with affection, a collection of fragrant herbs, whether in a window box or a rural field, will provide agreeable pleasures that delight all the senses.*

*Step into a world of extended sense-awareness: enlarge your vision, tantalize your tastebuds, amplify your hearing, remove your gloves and relax into a kaleidoscope of fragrances.*

ABOVE: *Purple Sage: a herb for all the senses offering colourful, textured, aromatic leaves with culinary, medicinal, cosmetic, aromatherapy and household uses.*

# Light & Shade

With all our senses pleasurably engaged and inter-related in a garden, visual images are usually the first to lure us in, allowing fragrance then to cast its atmospheric spell. Light is the essence of all visual images, and in the greater picture it is its presence or absence, the light or the shade, that dominates our vision. Aesthetic pleasure comes from the interplay between light and shade.

To create contrast in areas of bright sunshine choose plants with large leaves or dense clusters of leaves, both of which will create areas of shade beneath or beside them. For contrast in shady areas place reflective shiny-leaved herbs such as those of Solomon's Seal (*Polygonatum multiflorum*) and Lily-of-the-Valley, or the white spotted leaves of Lungwort (*Pulmonaria officinalis*) and cream Bugle (*Ajuga reptans*), or white flowers that tolerate shade such as Wild Strawberry, white Violets, Ramsons (*Allium ursinum*) or the white form of Evening Primrose to highlight what light is available. White flowers that can be grown in semi-shade include Wood Avens (*Geum urbanum*), Sweet Cicely, white-flowered Jacob's Ladder (*Polemonium caeruleum*), Chervil, Sweet Rocket, white-flowered Comfrey and the beautiful Musk Mallow.

The contrast of light and dark can also be created by placing silver foliage next to dark green or purple leaves. Herbs boast a host of gorgeous silvers including the intensely silver Curry Plant and Santolinas, and the softer silver of Artemisias, Thyme 'Silver Posie', common Sage, most Lavenders and Dittany of Crete (*Origanum dictamnus*). There are also several grey or woolly-leaved herbs for contrast such as Marsh Mallow, Verbascum and Horehound though none of these are scented. All silver herbs contrast beautifully with the dark green of Yew, Rosemary, Winter Savory, Peppermint or Caraway Thyme (*T. herba barona*), and with the neat, bright green leaves of Box.

There is an excellent range of purple-leaved and purple-stemmed herbs. Curiously, purple-stemmed plants seem to stand up well in stormy weather. The tall purple stems of Sweet Joe Pye (*Eupatorium purpureum*) stay proudly erect in driving rain; Basil Mint, Eau-de-Cologne Mint, Black Peppermint and Red Raripila Mint also sport sturdy purple stems. Purple-leaved Sage is the hardiest of the Sage varieties and looks stunning with any silver herbs. Purple Basil, purple variegated Bugle 'Rainbow' and Bronze Fennel also offer their contrasting dark foliage for visual interest.

Light highlights the texture and shape of plants. Consider interesting silhouettes; the vertical spiked leaves of Orris, the Florentine Iris with its violet-scented root, and of the medicinal Yucca, spherical Allium flowers, Opium Poppy seed capsules, tall imposing Elecampane with its enormous leaves, and the almost tropical appearance of handsome Angelica.

(Above) Dramatic squares of Box-edged silver Santolina featured as a new rarity and elegant moth-repellent in Tudor herbals.
(Below) The stunning silver-green leaved *Artemisia ludoviciana* is the most decorative of the Artemisias.

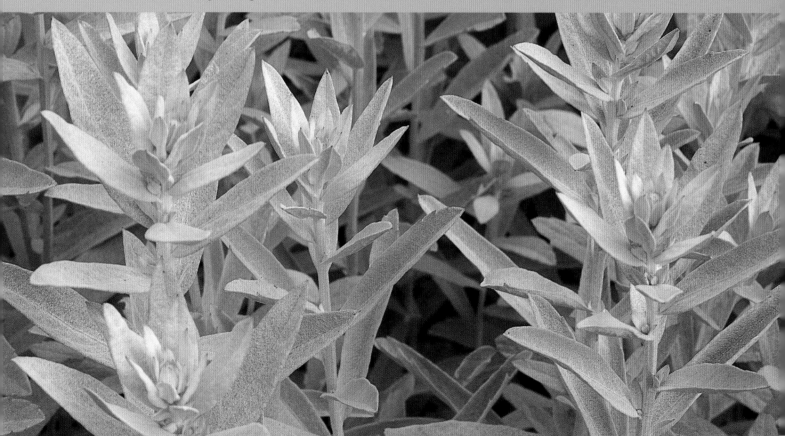

# Plant Colours

The flower colours of herbs have a natural elegance that creates harmonious blends in almost any combination. Because they are very close to wild species they do not share the garish appearance of some hybridized flowers and their natural exuberance brings charm to every garden.

Different colours can evoke different emotional responses and we can use this information to augment the power of fragrance to enhance chosen moods. This is not as intense an experience as colour therapy because each flower is surrounded by the calming and healing colour of green or silver leaves but a more intense response can be explored by picking several flowers to mass together, or by floating a selection of flowers in a small bowl and watching the changing patterns of colour.

The sunny colours of yellow, orange and white flowers, plus gold and variegated leaves, are wonderful assets in a refreshing, stimulating garden space. The old-fashioned Calendula or Pot Marigold flowers have a luminous gold or orange

unmarked by browns or other colours. Nasturtium petals share this colour intensity: the variety 'Alaska' has a range of flower colours from rusty magenta through orange to apricot and has cream marbled leaves. *Coreopsis tinctoria* is another herb with satin orange petals. There are many yellow herb flowers ranging from the pale yellow of Primrose through the butter yellow of Cowslip and Evening Primrose to the deep gold of St. John's Wort, source of the most popular herbal drug for the gloom of sunshine deficiency in winter. Tansy, Santolina and Curry Plant have acid yellow flowers; Ginger Mint, Golden Lemon Balm, Golden Marjoram and Gold Variegated Sage have leaves splashed with gold. The white daisies of Chamomile, Alecost, Pyrethrum (*Tanacetum cinerariifolium*) and Camphor plant (*Tanacetum balsamita* var. *champhoratum*) add further cheer.

The clear red and pink herbal flowers are perfect for a romantic garden. There are Roses from pale

ABOVE: *The sunshine-bright flowers of Feverfew which sports green and gold foliage forms.*

LEFT: *The sharp yellow flowers of Holy Flax (*Santolina viridis*) with their clean, pungent scent.*

angelic pink like 'Celestial' to deep passionate scarlets like 'Guinée'. Lush Peonies can be obtained in a similar colour range though most are not scented. Sweet Peas, pink Musk Mallow, Clove Pinks, Honeysuckle 'Repens' – with pink flowers and purple stems – and the pale lilac of Sweet Rocket each add romantic charm. Pink colours are intensified by the presence of blues such as the wild Geranium, Harebell or Borage and by the contrast of white flowers like Lilies, white Lilac and Jasmine.

Blues and purples are relaxing, meditative colours. To the blues listed above one could add the pale blue of Rosemary, Flax (*Linum usitatissimum*) and Chicory, the mid-blue of Alkanet, Virginia Skullcap (*Scutellaria lateriflora*) and Jacob's Ladder, the deeper blue of poisonous Monkshood (*Aconitum napellus*), Viper's Bugloss (*Echium vulgare*), Lungwort and Larkspur (*Consolida ambigua*) and finally the stunning rich blue of False Indigo (*Baptista australis*), a potent immune booster. For the colour range of blue-purple to purple there are Columbines (*Aquilegia vulgaris*), Hyssop, Catnip, Thymes, Sweet Violet, Foxglove and, of course, the wide variety of Lavenders.

For those very sensitive to colour it can be an evocative experience to pick a range of clear bright hues and place them on a flat surface in rainbow order. A selection picked on the day of the solar eclipse of August 1999 included scarlet Rose petals, vermillion Poppy petals, orange Nasturtium, gold Calendula, yellow-green Feverfew leaves, mid-green Crisp Tansy leaves, blue Borage, indigo Pansy flowers and deep purple Hidcote Lavender. As the sun re-emerged they seemed to glow in the new light. Each leaf or petal was a pure colour without other colour markings to reduce the intensity. Playing with colours in this way can provide new ideas for creating welcoming, invigorating, relaxing or simply beautiful colour combinations.

RIGHT: *Blue Jacob's Ladder, red Poppies and dusty-pink Clary Sage, with deep pink Wood Betony and white Horehound in the foreground. Note how the blue fades into the background while the bright red leaps forward.*

ABOVE: *Edible flowers make any dish magical: orange Calendula petals glisten in salad oil; Nasturtium flowers decorate shellfish; Salad Rocket flowers add visual interest and textural pleasure, and delight the taste buds. Use the flowers of old favourites like Rosemary, Thyme and Sage where a mild version of their flavour would be enjoyed, such as when added to the sugar for fruit salads.*

# Gourmet Gardens

As our flavouring repertoire is extended, through wider travel and a developing ethnic interest, the range of culinary herbs to grow in our gardens or window boxes increases. At the same time we continue to discover new reasons for cultivating old favourites.

## Culinary Favourites

Traditional English cooking invokes Parsley, the universal garnish and the 'summation of all things green'; it also invokes Chives, whose slender blades belie their sharp onion bite, for use in summer salads and soups; clean refreshing Mint bubbling with new potatoes; resinous Rosemary roasting with spring lamb; spicy Bay leaves with game and 'prima donna' Sage to flavour pork, duck and sausages while doubling as a digestive agent for these rich meats.

### HISTORICAL RECIPES

Historical recipes have kindled interest in half-forgotten flavourings which are perfect for the gourmet garden. From Tudor banquets Juniper berries season game and poultry marinade. To produce berries in your own garden it is necessary to grow both a male and female Juniper shrub. The beefy-celery taste of Lovage flavours broths and chicken, and Wild Celery or Smallage is cooked in soups and stews. Apicus' first century Roman Cookery Book lists an extraordinary range of herb flavourings once used in Britain, including Alecost, Asafoetida (*Ferula asafoetida*), Catmint, Myrtle berries, Safflower (*Carthamus tinctortius*), Spikenard and Sumach from the small tree *Rhus syriacum*. Grandmother's recipe book might reveal milk puddings flavoured with scented Geraniums and acid fruits cooked with Sweet Cicely to reduce the sugar needed. High profile chefs have revived the Elizabethan use of Lavender as a seasoning for vinegars and home-made ice cream.

## Travel Connections

For Mediterranean dishes save your sunniest positions to grow the warm flavours of spicy Basil, Garlic, Sweet Marjoram and Oregano for sauces and pizzas. Grow Thyme to flavour the wine used to simmer shellfish and poultry, tangy Tarragon to flavour chicken and vinegars, and refreshing Lemon Balm to add to oils, vinegars and fruit salads.

From Scandinavia and Eastern Europe comes an appreciation of aromatic Dill. The best flavour is in the flower-heads which are only available from the garden. Dill seeds flavour bread and apple pie, and Dill leaves complement the 'celebration fish', salmon. The history of breath-sweetening Caraway seeds reaches back to stone-age meals and cheeky Paprika, whose colour is stronger than its bite, features in goulash, pickles and cheese. Fennel adds aniseed hints to salads and fish; subtle musky-green, anise-flavoured Chervil, one of the French *fines herbes*, garnishes and flavours delicate dishes. Sorrel gives zest to Russian soups, Angelica stems are cooked as vegetables or have their sharp flavour tempered by crystallization, and Horseradish (*Armoracia rusticana*) has metamorphosed from a smoked fish and chicken condiment in the East to the traditional flavouring for roast beef in England.

Spanish and Arabian dishes have renewed the popularity of Saffron – the three orange stigmas from the autumn flowered Saffron crocus – which was grown commercially in Medieval England when its strange rich, earthy flavour was a luxury. Traditional paella, bouillabaisse and Cornish cakes are joined by new dishes as Saffron flavours fish, poultry, beef, breads and even ice cream. Thai ingredients for

Purslane (*Montia perfoliata* and *Portulaca oleracea*), Cress (*Lepidium sativa*), young leaves of Purple or Green Orach (*Atriplex hortensis*), garlic-flavoured Jack-by-the-Hedge (*Alliaria petiolata*) and Purple or Green Perilla [Shiso] (*Perilla frutescens*). A selection also provides a treasure chest of vitamins and minerals. Try fern-like Salad Burnet with its mild cucumber taste or tender young leaves of Good King Henry 'Netherfield Gold' (*Chenopodium bonus-henricus*) to frame a salad dish. Add small pieces of Angelica, Basil, Lovage, Sorrel or Nasturtium leaves, or feathery bits of Fennel, Dill or Asafoetida for a full complement of flavour.

BELOW: *Grow Wild Garlic to add its young leaves to salads or sandwiches and use the flower heads as a garnish, especially with Chinese dishes. Its powerful scent can dominate a woodland in spring while the shiny leaves and bright white flowers bring light to shady corners.*

soup, fish and chicken dishes include Lemon Grass to grow on your kitchen window, and Galangal root (*Alpinia galanga*) to grow in the conservatory.

Curry flavourings include Coriander seed, Cumin, Fenugreek (*Trigonella foenum-graecum*) and Chilli which can be grown in sheltered gardens or a greenhouse, and Ginger which can be grown from sprouted rhizomes in a conservatory, where it may reward you with a scented flower. Coriander's strangely pungent leaves, also called Cilento, make a vital contribution to Indian, Arabian and South American cuisine. The elusive secret of certain Indian vegetable dishes is Asafoetida, a perennial umbelliferae which will survive outdoors in cooler climates if sheltered. A pungent gum is extracted from its living roots and used in minute amounts for its unique sulphurous garlic flavour.

## Salad & Garnish Herbs

Salads are now an adventurous and nutritional delight. A crisp lettuce or chicory usually forms the base of a leaf salad, with accents chosen from Parsley, Salad Rocket (*Arugala*), Coriander leaf, young Spinach leaves, Chervil, Winter and Summer

# *Natural Sounds*

The drone of the buzzing bee, the uplifting sound of birdsong and the soft purring of a lazy cat, all have a soporific effect upon the senses reminiscent of hazy summer days. To encourage these sounds into your garden, choose herbs that are attractive to wildlife, and add an extra dimension with the soft, calming sound of trickling water.

## *An Enclosed Garden*

A garden with a protective surround of greenery (see page 46) not only concentrates plant perfumes but reduces noise pollution, often an unrecognized stress in daily life. The enclosed space allows the softer sounds of rustling leaves and gently bouncing raindrops to work their relaxing magic.

BELOW: *Encourage the busy drone of pollinating bees by planting their garden favourites.*

### *Bee Gardens*

An enclosed garden also allows bees to continue to work when windy conditions might otherwise halt their activity. Encouraging the bees benefits the pollination of plants and honey production, and reduces stress as their hypnotic drone drifts around the garden. Bees are more attracted by colour than scent. They like yellow, blue-green to blue, mauve, purple, and red containing ultraviolet. Grow bee plants in a sheltered position (Holly or Ivy on trellises also offer nectar), in full sun in groups of five or more, and include a range to flower from early spring to late autumn, which is helpful to the vanishing bumblebees. Beehives are better suited to large gardens, as bees ignore plants within about 15 m (50 ft) of their hive which may be contaminated by the bees' own cleansing flights.

**AROMATIC BEE PLANTS**
Anise Hyssop, Allium, Basil, Lemon (Bee) Balm, Borage, Catmint, Chamomile, Clover, Cowslip, Fennel, fruit tree blossom, Lime blossom, Marjoram, Meadowsweet, Melilot, Mignonette, Mint, Mustard, Nasturtium, Peony, Sage, Savory, Thyme, Valerian, Violet, Woodruff.

**NON-AROMATIC PLANTS**
Calendula, Crocus, Flax (*Linum usitatissimum*), Forget-me-not (*Myosotis sylvatica*), Ivy (*Hedera helix*), Jacob's Ladder (*Polemonium caeruleum*), Mullein (*Verbascum thapsus*), Phacelia (*Phacelia tanacetifolia*), Poppy (*Papaver* species), Sunflower (*Helianthus annus*), Teasel (*Dipsacus fullonum*), Woad (*Isatis tinctoria*), Winter Aconite (*Eranthis* species).

## *Other Wildlife*

The range of herbs above will also attract the hum of other insects: dragonflies with their brilliant dash of iridescent blue are drawn to the tall, vertical stems of Mullein and Sunflower, and aphid-eating hoverflies will reproduce faster on the rich nectar of Phacelia. Frogs love the cool moisture under large-leafed ground cover plants like Lungwort (*Pulmonaria officinalis*) and will add their characteristic sounds.

**BIRDSONG**
A shallow basin or bird bath of clean water attracts birds while the seed heads of several herbs, including Sunflower, Evening Primrose and Marjoram, provide a meal. Several herbal trees and shrubs also offer food, including the Bird Cherry (*Prunus padus*), Crab Apple (*Malus* species), Elder (*Sambucus nigra*), Holly (*Ilex aquifolium*), Honeysuckle (*Lonicera periclymenum*), Rowan (*Sorbus* species) and Yew (*Taxus baccata*).

**PURRING CATS**
Cats take great pleasure in wandering through the variety of plants in a herb garden. If the range includes Catnip (*Nepeta cataria*) you may find them blissfully nestled in the centre of the plant, inhaling the narcotic scent and purring gently. Catnip grown from seed *in situ* usually recovers from this attention but transplanted specimens may need protection. The

smaller Catmint (*Nepeta mussinii*), with its mildly fragrant spikes of lavender-blue flowers, also delights cats, but less intensely. Valerian, reported to be the real decoy of the Pied Piper, similarly attracts both feline pets and rodents, but the scent of the root reflects its odorous medieval name, 'Phu'.

## Breezes

Tinkling through wind chimes, hanging crystals or bells, the breeze brings unexpected light melodies to the garden. In ancient China kites were made using a frame around parallel strings through which the wind played music. Another Chinese idea was to place a Banana palm under a window to hear the rain as it bounced between the large curved leaves. A similar effect can be obtained in temperate climates with the leaves of Elecampane (*Inula helenium*).

The leaves of many herbs rustle in the breeze creating a soothing background sound, especially grasses like the fibre-producing New Zealand Flax (*Phormium tenax*) and Bamboos like the medicinal Black Bamboo (*Phyllostachys nigra*). Several trees with herbal properties, including Birch, Eucalyptus, Pine and the Aspen (*Populus tremula*), produce an evocative range of sighing, whispering and swishing. The dried leaves of woodland Strawberry make an inviting crunch underfoot and release a pleasurable scent.

## Water

Water offers two avenues of sound: still and tranquil or moving and vibrant. Water trickling, cascading or tumbling is refreshing, cooling and stimulating; it sparkles and dances as it plays with light. Sound is created via a stream, small waterfall or fountain and each choice offers the chance to experiment. With cascading water the height, speed and angle can be changed in steps to create different tones which combine as harmonious chords. If a pond or pool is not possible, a water feature can be made with pebbles or rocks. Different jets will create a variety of sounds, from a continuous rush to a soft trickle.

Water still, peaceful and reflective in a pond, pool or even a shallow bowl, especially with a seat nearby, invites us to focus on the subtle occasional sounds of a tiny splash or ripple as a small creature moves in the water. A mirror of tranquil water reflects the sky and interacts gently with sunlight in slow golden ripples, but is at its most memorable when reflecting a silvery moon.

ABOVE: *Use a cat's natural love of Catnip to encourage your pet to join you in the garden for a lazy summer's afternoon; the sound of gentle purring can be one of the most effective stress-relieving sounds found in nature.*

LEFT: *Listen to the hazy summer sounds of insects, frogs and birds attracted by a placid pond and moisture-loving plants.*

# Texture & Touch

ABOVE: *The feathery leaves of Santolina and the white pom-poms of double-flowered Feverfew invite an investigative touch.*

RIGHT: *The knobbly texture of Lemon Balm, the veins of a Geranium leaf and the silky petals of Cowslip invite contact, while the drop of nectar found at the back of each flower offers a sweet taste.*

The garden textures of satin petals, velvet leaves, smooth stones and soft earth invite our touch, drawing us into more intimate contact with our natural surroundings. Texture adds pleasure and complexity to sight and sound as well as touch. Rain glistening on a flagstone path highlights its irregular surface, reflects light on neighbouring plants and engages our playful instincts by inviting a sharp splashing footfall. Position seductive textures near garden seats and consider a marble bowl of water, for birds and bees and human fingers to dabble in.

Continue tactile awareness with a smooth hardwood strip across the front of a chamomile seat (see page 52) for leg comfort. Greenery softens the appearance of hard materials; grow ivy along stone risers or mounds of Corsican Mint between paving bricks. Without the clothing of summer greenery, winter reveals more of the texture of bark, twigs, shiny evergreen leaves and garden structures. Yet texture is the most discreet of the visual influences and, as a great variety never overpowers the picture, incorporate as much texture as your imagination offers.

## Textural Tones

Like different colours and musical notes, different textures invoke different responses. The most sensuous are the velvety angora leaves of Marsh Mallow (*Althaea officinal*). the woolly leaves of Lamb's Ears (*Stachys byzantina*) of the woundwort family, and Scented Geranium leaves such as *Pelargonium odoratissimum* which reward touch with the scent of apple sauce. The silky petals of California Poppy (*Eschscholzia californica*) offer further tactile invitations. Enjoy fluffy dandelions and the soft down on Verbascum stems and leaves, once collected as pillow stuffing.

Prickly plants lure us with their don't-touch-me texture. Three stunning spiky, purple-flowered biennials are the Milk Thistle (*Silybum marianum*), the imposing Scotch Thistle (*Onopordum acanthium*) and the flower arranger's Teasel (*Dipsacus fullonum*) whose soft springy flower spikes contrast with the harsh spikes of the leaves. Another biennial, Viper's Bugloss (*Echium vulgare*), has soft blue flowers on prickly stems and seeds which attach themselves to passing animals. The rich purple thistle-like flowers of perennial Globe Artichoke (*Cynara scolymus*) are supported by prickly bracts but the flower filaments are beautifully soft. The short-lived perennial Sea Holly (*Erngium maritimum*) has spiny leaf lobes to deter those who would gather its mineral-rich root, a popular candied cough medicine and aphrodisiac in the eighteenth century. The sharp-needled Juniper shrub like the thorny Blackberry needs to be approached with caution, as picking their berries often involves a puncture to the skin.

There are also buds which are sticky with a protective wax or resin. Those of the Balsam Poplar tree can be picked in spring to add their balsamic scent to potpourri. Glandular hairs on the leaves and stem of Labdanum, the Mediterranean shrub *Cistus ladanifer*, exude sticky aromatic resin in summer heat which is collected for medicinal and perfume use. The aromatic waxy surface of Wax Myrtle berries (*Myrica cerifera*) is melted to make spicy balsamic-scented candles.

Squidgy plants have a playful attraction. Much like bubble wrap, the balloon vase of Water Hyacinth (*Eichhornia crassipes*) is very difficult to resist squelching. The crinkled surface of Lady's Mantle (*Alchemilla mollis*) and large Medicinal Rhubarb leaves or the formal ridges on some Hostas intrigue our fingers as we trace their patterns. And who can resist the peeling bark on Silver Birch or the Paperback Maple (*Acer griseum*).

Indulge your sense of touch whilst in the garden, whether in summer or winter; run your fingers up a feathery Fennel, down a velvety Marsh Mallow, across a flat Yarrow flower head; stroke a mound of Chamomile 'Treneague'; rattle a Poppy seed capsule; trigger the explosive spring of Crane's-bill's seed pods (*Geranium pratens*); press a spongy ball of Box and cup your hands around the small tickling flower globes of Chives.

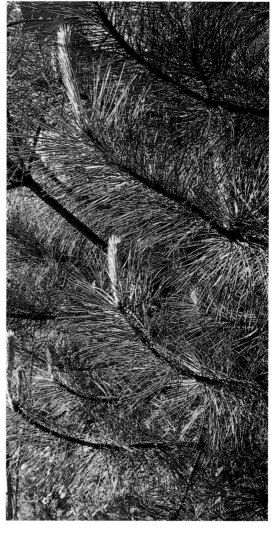

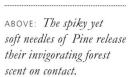
ABOVE: *The spiky yet soft needles of Pine release their invigorating forest scent on contact.*

ABOVE: *Grow tender herbs and rampant Mints in pots to place within stroking distance of the garden seat.*

OPPOSITE: *The lure of the garden path is enhanced by fragrant plants at foot level, hand height, nose height and above head height on the arch.*

# Fragrance

The concept of a scented garden holds universal appeal because, as a sixteenth-century essayist wrote, 'Sweet perfumes work immediately upon the spirits, for their refreshing and healthful ayres are special preservatives to health'. This perfumed place can be created in the garden or on a patio or balcony. The three primary ingredients are: a surround of fragrant plants at foot, hand and nose level and overhead on a pergola or in a hanging basket; a garden seat to encourage time to be taken to enjoy the scents (see pages 52–3); and finally some form of enclosure to create privacy and confine the perfumes (see pages 46–7).

For fragrant ground cover in a sunny area grow the non-flowering Lawn Chamomile (*Chamaemelum nobile* 'Treneague') with its apple-scented leaves, the new-mown-hay-scented Lady's Bedstraw (*Galium verum*), or one of the many creeping Thymes: *Thymus citriodorus*, *T.* 'Gold Variegated', *T.* 'Silver Lemon Queen', *T.* 'Doone Valley' and *T.* 'Lemon Curd' all have a lemony scent. *T. azoricus* has a resinous pine scent, *T. herba barona* has a caraway fragrance and most of the other Thymes, 'Annie Hall', *doerfleuri*,

*cochineal*, 'Snowdrift', 'Silver Posie' and *lanuguinosus* (woolly Thyme) share the familiar aroma of common Thyme. For a moist soil with semi-shade grow Pennyroyal or Corsican Mint (*Mentha requenii*) both sporting a strong Peppermint scent, Sweet Woodruff (*Galium odoratum*) with its hay scent, or Sweet Violets. The Lawn Chamomile, Pennyroyal and Thymes will take occasional foot traffic.

Explore the idea of flowery meads from Medieval times, a feature championed by William Robinson in the nineteenth century. These were sheltered areas of herbs and wild flowers where a lady could sit amongst the plants, reading her Book of Hours, strumming a lute or entertaining a suitor. Choose plants from among those mentioned by Shakespeare, especially in *A Midsummer Night's Dream*: Cowslip for its lovely milky-breath aroma, Wild Thyme, Columbine, Harebell, Violet, Primrose, Wild Strawberry, Ox-eye Daisy, Adonis flower (*Anemone numerosa*), Clover, Lawn Daisy, Cuckoo-flower, Lady's Smock, Pansy and Poppy.

Pleasant scents for trailing hands include old cottage favourites like Lavender, Lemon Balm, Southernwood, Clove Pinks, pungent silver Santolina and raspberry-scented Soapwort called Bouncing Bet. Add Bergamot and Lemon Verbena from the New World to classical Rosemary, Sage, Marjoram and Mints positioned to encourage bees and butterflies.

For fragrance at nose height grow handsome Angelica for its vermouth-scented leaves, feathery Fennel for its aniseed fragrance, plus elegant White Mugwort (*Artemisia lactiflora*) and Canadian Clover (*Melilotus alba*) for their honey-vanilla scent. Add Madonna Lily, but be careful of the staining yellow pollen as you inhale its intoxicating perfume. If space allows include Lilac, Mock Orange, Sweet Myrtle and scented Buddleias, each contributing an aromatic pleasure when in season.

Tender varieties of container-grown herbs, such as Pineapple Sage and Spice Basils, can be placed next to seats for extra aromatic treats. For scent above head height grow herbs in hanging baskets or train climbing plants on a trellis, screen or wall (see pages 52–3). And finally smother the area with all varieties of Roses and you have the recipe for fragrant contentment.

# Welcoming & Romantic Gardens

## WELCOME

For a welcoming ambience, start from the garden gate with borders of low growing aromatic herbs spilling onto the entrance path. As they release their fragrance underfoot they bring a smile to the face of guests. Grow single or mixed rows of Basil, Bergamot, Catmint, Hyssop, Eau-de-Cologne Mint, Lavender, Lemon Balm, Pinks, Rosemary, Sage, Savory, Southernwood, Thymes or Wall Germander. By the front door, clipped Bays make jovial porch sentinels (see Topiary page 54) and a colourful door garland of lively herbs and bright flowers signals friendliness.

Use pot-grown herbs to create an aromatic passageway through the entrance hall. Choose from Bay, Lemon Verbena, Sweet Myrtle, the Scented-leaf Geraniums, the Incense Plant (*Calomeria amaranthoides*), the Australian Mint Bush (*Prosanthera* species), Balm of Gilead, Pineapple or Tangerine Sages, Sweet Thymes, Citrus shrubs or the tender Lavenders such as *L. dentata*.

For outdoor entertaining consider the medieval tradition of strewing fragrant herbs. Lay a carpet of leaves and small branches on an approach path, a porch or a verandah; sprinkle them on a deck, terrace or garden seating area. Choices include Alecost, Lavender, Lemon Balm, Lemon Verbena, Meadowsweet, Melilot, Mints, Mugwort, Rosemary, Sage, Southernwood, Sweet Cicely, Sweet Flag (*Acorus calamus*), Sweet Grass, Sweet Marjoram, Sweet Myrtle, Sweet Woodruff, Lemon Thyme (*Thymus fragrantissimus* or *T. odoratus*), Eucalyptus, Pine, Thuja or Cedar branches. Even clearing them away later is a pleasant fragrant task.

Bunches of fresh herbs and sweetly scented flowers have instant visual and aromatic appeal. They can be arranged in generous bucketfuls, loose informal bouquets or small, pretty posies to bring a sense of the garden indoors when entertaining.

For regular outdoor eating grow a raised bed of colourful salad and garnish herbs (see page 15) so that guests can pick their favourites. Keep a pot of Thyme near the barbecue to sprinkle on the coals for fragrant smoke and save Rosemary stems to use as satay or kebab skewers. Gardens can be lit with smouldering herb torches made of tightly wrapped dried fragrant herbs. They exude a subtle scent and the smoke of several herbs, including Basil, Mint, Pennyroyal and Tansy, will act as insect repellents.

Whatever the style of entertaining, a concord of enticing scents will encourage each guest to inhale the welcoming fragrance and to revel in the good food, the conversation and the laughter of friends.

## ROMANCE

A secluded garden offers an opportunity for the seductive perfumes of nature to work their magic on the human heart. And as ambrosial perfumes open the door to romance, so also romantic encounters put all our senses on high alert.

Begin with a beckoning path through a protective hedge. Keep the seat or reclining area hidden from view. A seat is vital as it offers a place to pause, play, unravel cloud shapes or count shooting stars in the

indigo sky; a place to intensify expectations. Along the route place aromatic plants like Chamomile and Peppermint underfoot to refresh bare feet, others like Lavender along the edge to indulge trailing hands, some at nose height like Sweet Peas and old fashioned Roses to invite immediate attention, and grow the large tropical Angelica to make you feel like Alice in Wonderland. Above, drifts of Wisteria will complete the enticing picture.

The wide range of fragrance for romance and seduction falls broadly into five groups. The light, floral scents are gentle and relaxing as they generate well-being and openness. The world's favourite of these is Rose, the universal symbol of love. Grow Rose 'Celestial' for its delicate, pure scent and 'Madame Isaac Pereire' for the strongest Rose perfume. Next favourite is the haunting bitter-sweet scent of Orange Blossom whose aphrodisiac reputation stems from its ability to reduce anxiety, valued in bridal bouquets. A similar scent is shared by the white flowers of Mock Orange (*Philadelphus* species), the evergreen Mexican Orange Blossom shrub (*Choisya ternata*) and by the evergreen leaves of Sweet Myrtle.

Voluptuous Peony blooms have a demure perfume, offered only to those who pause close by. Honey-

LEFT (TOP): *Roses, the first flower of romance and the favourite symbol of love.*

LEFT (MIDDLE): *White Lilacs offer a sweet fragrance which drifts across the garden, especially in the evening.*

LEFT (BOTTOM): *Honeysuckle has a strong pervasive perfume to delight during a summer night's stroll.*

suckle with its magnetic evening scent is a symbol of fidelity for its tenacious climbing grasp. Wisteria, Lilac, Sweet Violet, Lily-of-the-Valley, Gardenias and the delicious plummy, floral scent of white Osmanthus flowers (*Osmanthus fragrans*) contribute to this floral group.

The next group are the exotics, usually white flowers, with an intensely sweet and slightly unsettling perfume hinting at unknown excitement. First are the tantalizing white Lilies (*Lilium candidum*, *L. longiflorum* and *L. regale*). Their heady fragrance is shared by Hyacinth and several Narcissi including 'Cheerfulness'. The rich narcotic perfume of tropical Jasmine flowers radiates peak potency on warm evenings giving it the Indian name of 'Moonlight of the Groves'. The strongest of all perfumes is from the white flower of the tender Tuberose (*Polianthes tuberosa*) which can be cultivated in an unheated greenhouse. From tropical climates the small yellow flowers of Ylang Ylang exude a less tenacious Jasmine-like fragrance and, along the Riviera, Mimosa spreads its intoxicating aroma.

Well known as aphrodisiacs, the 'spicy' scents like Cinnamon and Cardamom are warm and stimulating and arouse circulation. Most are tropical plants but Cinnamon Basil leaves and Sweet Flag stems have a spicy cinnamon scent; old fashioned Pinks offer a rich clove scent and Coriander and Anise seeds provide something spicy to nibble.

The 'Woody and Earthy' tree, moss and fern scents are rich, resonant forest smells that suggest deeper connections and ancient rituals. Cedarwood is warm and reassuring. Patchouli, a tender annual with nettle-like leaves has an intense balsamic forest-floor odour. Oak Moss from pollution-free areas has a smoky leather scent. One of the oldest plants in cultivation, the Saffron Crocus, has a delicate perfume but the dried flower stigmas develop a strong scent with intriguing sweet-earthy undertones long considered an aphrodisiac.

'Musk' scents have an erogenous edge that can be unpleasant in overpowering doses, but tiny amounts create a suggestive, animal undercurrent. Elder, Blackcurrant and Valerian roots exhibit this muscatel-foxy note.

## *Relaxing Spaces for Harmony & Balance*

The perfect antidote to tension and stress is to step into a garden of sweet herbs and allow the cool, green fragrances to work their magic. Inhaling the relaxing scent of Lavender, the almond-scented froth of Meadowsweet and the innocent perfume of Sweet Peas offers a path back to equilibrium. The tranquillizing fragrance of these herbs is enhanced by their soothing pastel colours, velvet textures and the wildlife they attract, filling the garden with fluttering butterflies, iridescent dragonflies, droning bees and birdsong.

### HARMONIOUS HERB COMBINATIONS

Most herbs have an easy natural appearance that fits gracefully into a garden for relaxation. Traditional fragrances and images include silvery Lavender with its sweet-sharp scent intermingled with musky Catmint or scarlet Bergamot; white Musk Mallow and blue Borage flowering together; the pink of Roses intensified by Geranium 'Johnson's Blue'; Clove Pinks set among delicate blue Harebells and the violet spikes of Anise Hyssop rising elegantly through pungent silver Roman Wormwood or sweet feathery Southernwood. Tall spires of the yellow Straw Foxglove (*Digitalis lutea*) look glorious above the fern-like leaves of Crisp Tansy. The size of luscious Peony blooms is emphasized by contrasting clouds of dainty white Queen Anne's Lace (*Anthriscus sylvestris*) or Sweet Cicely umbels. Experiments in combining plants are simple and fun because herbaceous herbs are easy to transplant.

Spring offers sweetly aromatic Broom, Daphne and Wall Flowers. Late spring brings the honey-vanilla perfume of climbing Akebia's dangling purple flower clusters, with Lilac and the shy Sweet Violets. Midsummer wafts us the orange-blossom scent of Philadelphus (Mock Orange), Sweet Myrtle and Choisya (Mexican Orange Blossom). The feathery foliage of Lawn Chamomile releases its apple fragrance to wriggling toes on a summer's day while the earthy-green scented flowers provide a soothing tea to sip in the shade on hot afternoons. The tranquillizing flowering tops of Sweet Marjoram have a spicy green scent. In late summer, the penetrating warm nutty pungency of Clary Sage, emanating from its large textured leaves and dusty mauve, pink and lilac flowers, has powerful relaxing properties valued in aromatherapy. Later, the soothing honey

BELOW (LEFT): *Sweet Violets with their soft colour and unique, soothing floral scent.*

BELOW (RIGHT): *The intriguing, warm pungency of Clary Sage's flower bracts and leaves is deeply relaxing.*

sweetness of Buddlcia attracts butterflies. In the new year, winter-flowered Honeysuckle gives a delicately fragrant start to the year.

## EVENING AND MEDITATION SCENTS

When we have quiet reflective time, rich resinous aromas inhaled in the tranquillity of a garden will slow and deepen our breathing and return us to a state of peaceful contemplation. Ramon Llull the thirteenth century Catalan mystic 'found in trees and herbs a type of the divine potency by which the natural world might serve as a ladder to the spiritual'.

From earliest tribal campfires humanity has shared an uplifting well-being through the inhalation of the smoke of aromatic wood resins. This communal experience is acknowledged in the word 'perfume' *par fume*, which means 'by smoke'. To regulate this experience the balsamic resins, particularly those of Frankincense, Myrrh, Sandalwood, Benzoin (the wild Styrax tree) and Aloes wood (*Aquilaria* species) were made into incense for prayer and meditation still used by the major religions. In Germany research into Frankincense found that a person who inhales its burning aroma experiences a positive mind-shift in the brain. The uplifting and protective qualities of Cedar, Juniper, Pine, Rosewood and Copal (*Hynenaea courbaril*) are among others sacred to traditional cultures.

Resins are a tree's first-aid device with their own internal circulation system enabling them to travel quickly to any point in the tree that is attacked or wounded. To fulfil this role resins are antiseptic, anti-viral and anti-fungal which gives them legendary healing properties in addition to their relaxing, calming, uplifting qualities.

For a venerable meditative experience, the aromatic and spatial qualities of an ancient woodland or a sacred grove generate a deep sense of peace and protection. The sweet clean smells of damp earth, leaves, and moss; the fragrance of Primrose, Cowslips, Sweet Violets and Wild Strawberries; the gentle rustling of leaves and the infinite shades of green filtered light all nourish the mind and spirit and provide a sense of con-

tinuation and unity that brings the deepest peace.

A garden of relaxation herbs also contributes to a meditative state. Soft colours and the movement of plants in a breeze can help release the anxieties of the day. Sitting alone in the gentle fragrance, a change in perception can occur when the sun moves from behind a cloud and the eyes adjust to the increased light reflection on every leaf and petal, literally enlightening the garden. This process can disengage anxious thought patterns, move the mind into neutral and then allow fresh energy, sponsored by aromatic herbs, to flood the system, restoring internal balance and revealing new perspectives. These benefits increase each time we re-enter the garden as the memory of previous relaxation helps us return more quickly to a calm, harmonious state.

On warm summer nights a stroll in the garden invokes deep serenity: under the moon, silver leaves shimmer and white Lilies, white Peonies and the froth of Sweet Cicely and Meadowsweet flowers seem to be lit from within. The ethereal blues of the faintly scented Forget-me-not and Madonna-blue Borage appear to hover in the air. Deep indigo and purple starlit skies magnify night-scented flowers 'seen' with the nose, as drowsy Lilac, Honeysuckle and Mignonette drift across the night air.

To spend contemplative time in a garden a comfortable sheltered seat out of the wind reduces discomforting distraction, and for evening strolls consideration should be given to a safe, even path, perhaps with small solar-powered side lights. For frequent use consider the covered walkway often illustrated in ancient Chinese gardens. Then stroll or sit amongst the colours, fragrances and textures of your own sacred space.

ABOVE: *One of many species of tree whose aromatic resins provide the long-lasting scents valued in incense, with Sweet Peas, whose uplifting colour soothes the spirit.*

# PLANTING & POTTING

*Inspired by the sensuous potential of aromatic herbs we can consider the practical aspects of creating a fragrant herbal area that suits our circumstances. The available space, light and climate, the containers and compost, and the choice of herbal fertilizers and insecticides all enter the equation. Because herbs are so versatile, they offer the opportunity to generate a mood-enhancing atmosphere even in the tiniest space. Growing only a few herbs also encourages more intimate knowledge of the individual plants. While doing the physical work of tending aromatic plants we discover that even the routine tasks are enjoyable as fragrance fills the air around us. Finally, harvesting the crop for future culinary, household or beauty uses brings the anticipation of further pleasures to come.*

*Most herbs are easy to grow as they are un-hybridized wild plants. The trick is to provide their native conditions, especially the sunshine and drainage they are accustomed to. With care, herbs should thrive whether in pots or gardens.*

# Herb Gardening in Small Spaces

## Container-Grown Herbs

A collection of healthy pot-grown herbs and fragrant flowers conjures up the friendly image of an attentive gardener lovingly tending his or her plants and engaging in a neighbourly chat to exchange ideas and cuttings.

Growing herbs in containers extends both the choice of plants and the growing season. Mobility makes them useful for filling seasonal gaps with extra colour and fragrance, or concealing eyesores. The containers can also be repositioned to catch the sun or the eye of the barbecue chef. Tender plants can be brought indoors for protection over the winter, and decorative aromatics used as table decorations or to enliven a convalescent's room.

When designing an aromatic balcony or patio garden, consider all three dimensions, positioning fragrant plants at foot level (Pennyroyal, Corsican Mint, Lawn Chamomile and creeping Thymes); at fingertip height (Bergamot, Sweet Myrtle and Artemisias); at nose height (Angelica, Fennel, Dill and Roses); and above, with hanging baskets and climbers (Akebia, Roses, Honeysuckle and Jasmine). When checking for areas that are in sun and shade, remember to look up. Higher areas may catch the sun even when lower parts of a balcony or terrace are in shade. Multiple heights can be achieved with tiered blocks, tall pots, interlocking pots which form a wall, cantilevered brackets or beams, or trellis which gives the opportunity to grow scented climbers in a trough at the base. Both trellis and trough can be on castors to create a movable wall.

ABOVE: *Pots of refreshing Rosemary, Bay, Santolina and cut-leaf Wormwood are beautiful, useful and aromatic.*

### THE PLANTS

Given the correct conditions, most aromatic plants can be grown successfully in pots. Tall plants like Angelica and Fennel will require deep or weighty containers, or wall support, to prevent them from toppling over. Herbs like Parsley, Mints and Chervil, which prefer cooler soil, should not be allowed to dry out in hot sun; if possible, provide dappled sunlight for the plants or shade for their soil. Soft-leaved herbs like Basil and tall plants will be damaged by winds, so provide windbreaks with dense netting, trellis or evergreen shrubs, and avoid placing tall plants or hanging baskets on exposed roof gardens or in the 'wind tunnels' which can occur between buildings and walls.

### THE CONTAINERS

Clay pots are aesthetically pleasing, stable and allow excess water to evaporate though their surface, but they also cause plants to dry out more quickly. Soak new clay pots in water for 24 hours before use. Plastic pots are cheaper, easier to clean and store, and lighter, which is useful for balconies and roof gardens. All types of containers need drainage holes, and all plants will benefit from a layer of gravel or broken crocks in the bottom to prevent waterlogging. Consider using interesting and unusual outer containers for your herb collection: try wicker baskets and wooden trugs, ornamental bird cages, copper kettles, tureens, brightly painted tins and modern pottery.

In general, the larger the pot, the better the crop, especially with lush-leaved plants like Basil. Annuals grown for their leaves, such as Rocket and Coriander, may bolt to seed if their growth is restricted and, like taprooting herbs such as Borage and Dill, will perform better in deep pots. Herbs can be started in 8–11.5 cm (3–4½ in) pots and moved in stages to 15–30 cm (6–12 in) pots. Subshrubs like Lavender and Rosemary should finish in 25–30 cm (10–12 in) pots. Roses, clipped Bay, Citrus trees, Lovage, Fennel and Angelica will grow well in a Versailles box or half-barrel, and in these Lemon Verbena will develop to its full 3 m (10 ft) magnificence.

Herbs can be grown in a variety of containers and in combinations for different uses. Here a blend of cottage herbs, including Marjoram, Thyme and Sage, tumble 'in sweet profusion' out of a strawberry pot (top left); the bright green of curled Parsley and Mint, the lively green and gold of Variegated Lemon Balm leaves and the cheerful orange-gold flowers of Calendula enliven a breakfast patio (top right); for greater convenience a selection of herbs including flat-leaf Parsley, green and Tricolor Sage, Mint and Marjoram are grown at hand height near the kitchen and barbecue with Golden Feverfew to supply a year-round splash of gold (bottom left); a painted two-tier stand houses culinary herbs including Parsley, Purple Sage, Chives, Basil and Mints (bottom right).

# Herb Companions

When planting your crops, refer to this table. 'Friends' will either encourage plant growth or deter pests. 'Enemies' are detrimental to healthy growth and flavour purity.

## Angelica
FRIEND Parsley
ENEMIES Celery; Lovage

## Apple
FRIENDS Mint; Nasturtium – *grow up and around trunks to deter woolly aphids*; Alliums (especially Chives) – *help protect against scab*; Penstemon – *can repel sawfly*; Tansy – *discourages moths*

## Artichoke
FRIEND Parsley
ENEMY Garlic

## Basil
FRIEND Parsley
ENEMIES Rue; Tansy; Artemisias

## Beans
FRIENDS Savory; Borage; Buckwheat; Phacelia – *attract hoverflies*; Elder – *leafy twigs deter blackfly*
ENEMY Alliums

## Bergamot
FRIEND Mint; Parsley; Brassicas

## Brassicas
FRIENDS Mint, Hyssop, Sage, Thyme, Dill, Caraway – *strong scents help confuse predatory insects*; Bergamot – *strewn between young brassicas deters flea beetles*; Nasturtium – *deters whitefly*
ENEMIES Beans; Tomato

## Carrot
FRIENDS Onion; Garlic; Wormwood; Sage; Rosemary; Chives; Coriander; Tomato; Radish; Lettuce – *strongly scented herbs confuse carrot fly, others improve carrot health*

## Catmint
FRIENDS Thyme; Radish

## Chamomile
ENEMY Rue

## Chervil
FRIENDS Radish; Beans
ENEMY Rue

## Courgette
FRIENDS Nasturtium; Borage; Fennel
ENEMY Rue

## Cucumber
FRIEND Borage
ENEMIES Thyme; Sage

## Dill
FRIEND Brassicas
ENEMY Carrot

## Fennel
FRIENDS Courgette; Marrows
ENEMIES Most other plants

## Fig
FRIEND Rue

## Garlic
FRIEND Beetroot; Strawberry
ENEMY Legumes

## Grape
FRIENDS Blackberry; Sage; Mustard; Hyssop – *increases yields*

## Hyssop
FRIEND Brassicas

## Lavender
FRIENDS Thyme; Marjoram
ENEMIES Rue; Parsley

## Lemon Balm
ENEMIES Rue; Fennel

## Lettuce
FRIEND Chervil – *deters aphids, ants and possibly slugs*

## Marjoram
ENEMY Alliums

## Mint
FRIEND Nettle

## Parsley
FRIEND Lavender

## Peach
FRIENDS  Alliums – *also for apricot*; Strawberry – *host to parasites which feed on oriental fruit moths*

## Pear
FRIENDS  Tansy; Mint; Nasturtium

## Plum
FRIENDS  Legumes – *help maintain mineral levels*; Garlic – *aids general tree health*

## Potato
FRIENDS  Beans; Maize; Nasturtium; Summer Savory; Flax; Comfrey – *wilted leaves planted with seed potatoes prevent scab*; Horseradish – *buried in perforated pots to contain its vigour, deters eelworms*; Marigold – *Tagetes deters eelworms.*
ENEMIES  Black and Woody Nightshade

## Radish
FRIENDS  Nasturtium; Chervil

## Raspberry
FRIENDS  Garlic; Rue; Tansy; Marigold (*Tagetes*)

## Rose
FRIENDS  Chives – *control blackspot, but can take three years to become effective*; Sage, Garlic, Parsley – *deter aphids (do not allow Garlic to flower)*; Spearmint – *deters aphid 'owners', ants*

## Rosemary
FRIENDS  Sage; Brassicas; Beans

## Sage
FRIENDS  Brassicas; Carrot; Rosemary

## Southernwood
FRIEND  Brassicas

## Strawberry
FRIENDS  Borage; Catnip – *can reduce bird damage, but a sacrificial clump in sun is needed if there are cats in the area.*
ENEMY  Brassicas

## Summer Savory
FRIEND  Beans
ENEMY  Radish

## Sweet Pepper
FRIEND  Basil

## Tarragon
FRIEND  Potato
ENEMIES  Fennel; Rue

## Thyme
FRIENDS  Rose; Brassicas
ENEMY  Rue

## Tomato
FRIENDS  Mint; Basil, Onion, Chives – *deter insects; Tagetes* Marigold – *deters white fly, and roots excrete a nematode-killing substance. Grow with Basil;* Asparagus – *root secretions kill tomato root nematodes, while tomatoes deter asparagus beetles. Grow with Parsley;* Dandelion – *exudes cichoric acid which protects tomatoes from fusarium wilt disease;* Nettle – *helps tomatoes keep longer;* Borage – *can reduce attacks of tomato hornworms;* Horehound – *stimulates fruiting,* Nasturtium – *deters whitefly from greenhouses and acts as a sacrifice to black aphids*
ENEMIES  Brassicas; Potato

## Winter Savory
FRIEND  Beans
ENEMY  Radish

## Wormwood
*Plant Wormwood and other Artemisias in their own bed, as they inhibit the growth of many plants and can even discourage earthworms*

## Yarrow
ENEMY  Rue

# *Useful Garden Herbs*

Pungent herbs are a boon to the organic gardener, as their chemical make-up can reduce or eliminate many potential horticultural problems. Some herbs supply fertilizer and green manure, while others deter pests and diseases or encourage beneficial insects.

## *Herbal Fertilizers*

To brew a general fertilizer with extra potash, pack chopped Comfrey or Nettle leaves into a container, cover with water, add a lid (it will smell dreadful) and soak for four weeks. Use the liquid fertilizer as needed by diluting 20:1 with water. It is especially good for tomatoes, potatoes and houseplants. Yarrow, another good general fertilizer, also provides extra copper.

Dill tops are rich in minerals, potassium, sulphur and sodium; Fenugreek sprouted seeds provide nitrates and calcium; Tansy leaves supply potassium and several minerals; and brewed Tea leaves yield nitrogen, phosphoric acid, manganese and potash.

BELOW: *Comfrey provides an excellent potash fertilizer with calcium, potassium, phosphorus and trace minerals. Yarrow makes a good general, copper-rich version.*

To use as fertilizer in the garden, pour 1 litre (2 pints) boiling water over 1 cup fresh or ½ cup dried herb, cover and steep for ten minutes, then strain and water needy plants.

### GREEN MANURE

Growing a green manure crop for one season will increase fertility and improve the texture of the soil. Phacelia (*Phacelia tanacetifolia*) is an excellent blue-flowered annual to use; scatter seed thinly over the area to be treated and dig in at the flowering stage.

### COMPOST ACTIVATOR

When adding fresh greenery to a compost heap, Yarrow works homoeopathically to activate decomposition. Use one finely chopped leaf for each wheelbarrow-load of compost material.

## *Herbal Insecticides*

Among plants which eliminate harmful insects, the Neem Tree is destined for world importance. Following its crop of fragrant white flowers are seeds which yield the potent, but non-toxic, garlic-scented Margosa oil that can destroy over 200 insect species including locusts, grasshoppers, cockroaches and rice pests, plus mites, nematodes, fungi, bacteria and some viruses. When purchasing, ask suppliers for Neem products.

Derris powder (from *Derris elliptica*, and best purchased with instructions) is used to control biting and sucking insects, especially aphids, but must be kept away from ponds as it is harmful to frogs and fish. Pyrethrum powder, from the pretty, mildly pungent white daisy, is another to use on sucking insects. Buy it ready-made, or grow your own plants, dry and powder the flowerheads, and sprinkle where required (wearing gloves) to deter flies, ants, cockroaches, bedbugs and fleas. For garden use, steep 55 g (2 oz) powder in 75 ml (⅛ pint) methylated spirit, dilute with 27 litres (6 gallons) water and spray.

When using herbal insecticide treatments, aim to do so late in the day, preferably in the evening, to cause the least possible harm to beneficial insects, bees and butterflies.

### APHID CONTROL

To control aphids, pour 1 litre (2 pints) boiling water over four crushed garlic cloves, cover and steep for ten minutes. Strain, cool, add 1 tsp washing-up liquid to help it stick to the leaves and use it as a spray the same day.

### GREENHOUSE PESTS

Sprinkled prunings of antiseptic herbs like Thyme, Rosemary, Sage, Wormwood, Hyssop, Savory and Bay will discourage pests from the greenhouse.

### 'BIOLOGICAL' CONTROL

Hoverfly larvae consume enormous quantities of greenfly. To encourage them in your garden, grow Phacelia, Buckwheat, Geranium (*Geranium* species), Chamomile, Dill, Fennel, Heliotrope, Marigold, Mint, Nasturtium, Parsley, Poppy, Sunflower, Sweet Rocket and Yarrow.

## *Antifungal Herbs*

To prevent damping-off mould in seedlings, pour 1 litre (2 pints) boiling water over 1 cup fresh (or ½ cup dried) Chamomile flowers, cover and steep for ten minutes. Strain, cool and water over seedlings the same day.

To combat mildew and fungal diseases, prepare a mixture as above but using Couch Grass rhizomes instead of Chamomile flowers.

## *Companion Planting*

Chamomile is called the 'Physician Plant' as it improves the health of most plants grown nearby, possibly by exuding a plant tonic through its roots. Foxglove has a similar effect.

Some smells confuse or deter aroma-sensitive insects. The female carrot fly can smell bruised carrot leaves 6.5 km (4 miles) away and home in to lay her eggs, but stems of pungent Wormwood left next to a carrot row will mask the carrot scent as they are stepped on while the gardener tends the crop. Garlic will deter many pests, as will the *Tagetes* Marigolds, which are excellent grown between tomato plants, while Tansy benefits orchards.

**(Above) Tread strongly scented Wormwood clippings while weeding to deter carrot fly. (Below) Root secretions from *Tagetes* deter potato eelworms.**

# Propagating Herbs

## Seed

Seed can be sown directly into the ground if the soil has been prepared to a fine tilth. Sowing *in situ* is best for the annual umbellifers (Aniseed, Chervil, Dill, Coriander and Cumin, and biennial Parsley), as transplanting may cause them to run to seed before they have produced a useful crop of leaves. Suitable for:

ANNUALS Aniseed, Basil, Borage, Calendula, Chamomile (annual), Chervil, Coriander, Cumin, Dill, Mustard, Nasturtium, Opium poppy, Orach, Purslane, Salad Rocket, Summer Savory, Sweet Marjoram.

BIENNIALS Angelica, Caraway, Parsley (curled and broad-leaf), Smallage (Wild Celery), Woad.

PERENNIALS Chamomile (perennial, flowering), Chives, Fennel (green and bronze), Feverfew, Good King Henry, Lovage, Marjoram (French), Oregano, Rue, Sage, Salad Burnet, Sorrel, Sweet Cicely, Thyme (common), Welsh onion, Wormwood.

## Cuttings

A healthy parent plant is important for good-quality cuttings. The younger the parent plant, the more easily the cuttings will root. Suitable for:

Bay (with heat), Box, Curry Plant, Hyssop, Lavender, Lemon Verbena, Marjoram, Pelargonium, Rosemary, Rue (*Ruta graveolens* 'Jackman's Blue'), Sage, Santolina, Tarragon (French), Thyme, Winter Savory, Wormwood (cultivars).

## Root Sections

This is the easiest form of propagation. Take 5–10 cm (2–4 in) pieces of root, each with growing buds, and plant approximately 2.5 cm (1 in) deep in a pot of compost. Longer pieces are better if you are planting straight into the ground. Suitable for:

Bergamot, Mint, Soapwort, Sweet Woodruff.

## Root Cuttings

A few herbs, such as Horseradish, Comfrey and Skirret, can be propagated from thick pieces of root 5–7.5 cm (2–3 in) long. Make a neat cutting, with the top flat and the bottom sloping so that you will remember which way is up, and insert vertically into potting compost topped with a 6 mm (¼ in) layer of sand.

## Division

Many herbs can be divided by digging up the plant, preferably in autumn or spring, and carefully separating the sections, each with a growing point and some roots. Replant or pot up, and water until the roots have re-established themselves. Some plants, such as Lovage, can be sliced vertically through the thick root, ensuring that each piece has a growing top.

Bulbous plants such as Chives and Everlasting Onion can be pulled apart in the same manner and replanted.

Aloe Vera produces offshoots (mini plants around the base) which can be removed carefully in summer, left to dry for a day and then replanted in sandy compost. Suitable for:

Alecost, Bistort, Camphor Plant, Chamomile (Lawn), Cowslip, Elecampane, Good King Henry, Lemon Balm, Lungwort, Marjoram, Meadowsweet, Primrose, Skirret, Sorrel, Sweet Joe Pye, Sweet Violet, Tansy, Tarragon (French), Wall Germander, Wormwood (Roman).

# Harvesting & Drying Herbs

Herbs should be dried slowly, away from sunlight and humidity, to preserve their properties. Use a well ventilated cupboard with a drying temperature of 32°C (90°F) for the first 24 hours, and 24–26°C (75–80°F) thereafter; cooler temperatures lengthen the drying time. Store dried herbs in dark-coloured, airtight glass jars labelled with the name of the herb and the date, placed out of direct sunlight. Condensation indicates that the lid is not airtight or that the herb is not fully dried. Most herbs are best used within a year.

### LEAVES

Best harvested just before the plants flower, leaves can be picked for immediate use at any time during the growing season. Collect undamaged leaves after the morning dew has evaporated. Cut whole stems of small-leaved herbs such as Marjoram and Thyme. Try to wipe, not wash, soil from leaves. Hang stems of small-leaved herbs in small, loose bunches tied with string. Spread larger leaves thinly over muslin or pierced brown paper stretched over wire cooling racks. Dry pungent herbs away from others to avoid tainting.

### FLOWERS

Harvest undamaged flowers when they are just fully open; collect in an open basket late in the morning in dry weather, when the dew has evaporated and the sun has begun to warm the blooms. Take care not to bruise the petals as you pick. Dry small-headed flowers such as Chamomile whole, but separate the petals of larger flowers and dry as for leaves. Small quantities can be dried in microwave ovens – dry in single layers on low or medium power for 6–20 minutes depending on the thickness of the petals, turning at 2–3-minute intervals. This is also a useful test of colour retention for petals intended for potpourri.

### SEEDS AND FRUITS

Collect papery-dry ripe seed on a warm, dry day before it disperses. Collect pods directly into paper bags, keeping species separate and labelled. Pick ripe fruit before it is overly soft. Collect berries and hops on their stalks and remove when half dried. Remove seeds from pods and place in a drying cupboard or warm, dry room, spread out in boxes with identifying labels. Umbels of seeds can be hung up by their stems to fall into boxes, or tied loosely in paper bags. Seeds will usually dry within two weeks. Seed for sowing should be kept in labelled paper envelopes in a cool, dark, frost-free place. Dry Rosehips and fruits in an airing cupboard, turning them frequently.

### ROOTS AND RHIZOMES

Dig up roots and rhizomes in autumn, after the aerial parts of the plant have begun to wither and die. Perennial roots are harvested in their second or third year. Always check the legality of harvesting the roots of wild plants – in Britain, it is illegal to harvest roots from any land except your own without the owner's permission. Clean them and cut large ones into smaller pieces. Dry slowly in an oven at 50–60°C (120–140°F), turning regularly until fragile and easily broken. Store in dark-coloured, airtight containers, and discard if the roots become soft. Orris root needs to be turned occasionally, but must be left in a drying cupboard for at least three years to develop its proper scent.

BELOW: *After the dew has evaporated and the sun has begun to warm the blooms, spend a leisurely morning in the garden harvesting Lavender and Marjoram.*

*Successful garden design is a considered mix of practical and inspirational ideas blended to create a chosen effect. In garden design more than anything, the whole is most definitely greater than the sum of the parts.*

# Planning the Garden

## Choosing the Site

When planning a garden from scratch it is best to first assess all the advantages of the space. If possible choose a site with at least three-quarters of the area in sunlight to give scope for the greatest variety of herbs. Many popular aromatic plants like Rosemary, Thyme, Sage, Lavender, Hyssop and Basil are of Mediterranean heritage and yearn for sunshine and sharp drainage. Those from cooler climates such as Mint, Fennel, Angelica, Lovage, Chives and Sweet Cicely appreciate the cool moist air and will tolerate some shade. In the northern hemisphere a south facing slope is ideal as the ground will be warmer and provide better drainage. For the southern hemisphere, aim for a north facing slope.

BELOW: *Fresh herbs delight the mind and the senses in the fragrant gardens of Wollerton Old Hall, Shropshire.*

## Soil & Site Preparation

Most herbs, like vegetables, prefer a slightly alkaline well drained soil but will tolerate a wide range of conditions from light sandy earth to heavy clay. If you are transplanting a container-grown herb into heavy soil, incorporate a child's size bucket of coarse sand or grit into the planting area to improve drainage. Coarse or horticultural sand has grains with facets and rough edges which create tiny air pockets in the soil allowing roots to penetrate more easily, oxygen and friendly bacteria to collect and water to drain away. Never use builder's sand as it has small smooth grains which fill the tiny air spaces, creating further problems. Clear the site of perennial weeds and put it into good heart by incorporating compost or leaf mould as this will produce healthy plants, and healthy plants are the most resistant to disease.

## Enclosure

For those lucky enough to have space for a separate herb garden it can be a place of enchantment. This feeling is emphasized if the area is enclosed by a hedge, wall or fence. A special entrance, such as an arch clipped into Yew or a circular Chinese moongate, reinforces the idea of stepping into a special place, heightening expectations and sense awareness.

Besides defining the area and declaring it a special space, a herb garden surround fulfils five further functions: it creates privacy; it provides shelter from buffeting winds for both humans and for bees and butterflies; it helps contain and concentrate the plant fragrances; it filters traffic sounds and other noise pollution; and it can block undesirable views. Yew is the classic hedge material because it clips beautifully and is a perfect dark green foil for the full range of herbal colours. Sweet Briar Rose, Shakespeare's Eglantine, provides a thick barrier with apple-scented leaves. Willow plants can be woven together to create a living fence with plant pockets, seats, arches and even arbours fashioned into the structure. If there is a desirable view outside your garden, cut a window shape in the hedge, fence or wall to accentuate this view in the Chinese manner of 'borrowed scenery'.

Along the southern boundary of the herb garden, to maintain the privacy but avoid the dense shade created by a wall or hedge, construct an open fence or a timber frame screen with a weave of diagonal ropes and train evergreen Honeysuckle or Ivy along the ropes.

When planning the height of a hedge, follow a photographer's guidelines and avoid a height which cuts the picture in half or cuts through the middle of your eye line. Plan to have it either higher, with the hedge filling two-thirds of the image allowing one-third sky, or lower, with one-third hedge and two-thirds sky. Allow 195 cm (6 ft 6 in) for the hedge height, up to 240 cm (8 ft) for an arched opening. Shaping the length of the hedge with sculptural curves changes it from a boundry into a work of art.

# Vertical Features

Using tall features to lift plants above eye level has a transforming effect in a garden. It brings scent and colour to the top of the picture as a living frame of greenery and accords the luxurious sensation of being lightly encompassed by Nature.

Hedges and fences contribute useful height but more specific vertical features can be introduced with a pergola, arbour, tripod, tall sculptures and screens. A cantilevered beam or an upright post can be positioned to conceal undesirable elements outside the garden's boundary. Foliage along the top of a pergola or arch will even mask the sight of a tall building.

Trees or tall herbs grown for their height and their aromatic or culinary properties can also be judicially positioned to reduce unsightly images. For the large garden a Lime tree will conceal almost anything, while the flowers perfume an entire neighbourhood and provide Lime blossom tea. Ash tree keys (seed cases) can be pickled and used like black olives on pizza. Young Beech leaves, tender enough to add to a salad, can be steeped in gin to create a brilliant green liqueur. For the smaller garden, musk-scented Elder, winter-flowered Witch Hazel, soft Willows and graceful Silver Birch all offer medicinal virtues. Of the evergreen herbs Bay, Sweet Myrtle, Juniper and Box can surpass 3 m (10 ft). The tall herbaceous herbs Sweet Joe Pye, Lovage, Elecampane with its shaggy yellow flowers, Goat's Rue (*Galega officinalis*), Fennel and Marsh Mallow can exceed human height. Tall biennials like Angelica and Scotch Thistle sometimes reach 3 m (10 ft), Mullein (*Verbascum thapsus*) and Teasel reach 2.2 m (7 ft) while the annual Sunflower can tower at 4 m (13 ft).

To train and support fragrant climbers fix a spiral of string or wire to posts. Annual climbers like Sweet Peas and Nasturtium will give instant summer appeal.

ABOVE: *This teepee of rustic canes will encourage the Sweet Peas to climb to the top and impart their delicate fragrance at nose height and above to drift around the garden.*

LEFT: *Train climbers along posts and arches to create a fragrant canopy. Choose from Roses, Honeysuckle, Jasmine, Akebia, Clematis, Hops and the unscented, but evergreen, Ivies.*

# Herbal Topiary

A garden approach with eye-catching shapes, cheerful colours and sweet scents creates a welcoming atmosphere while the aromatic garden makes a pleasant setting for entertaining. As a welcoming device, a clipped evergreen shape of Bay, Box, Lavender, Rosemary, Santolina, Savory, Sweet Myrtle, shrubby Thyme or upright Wall Germander creates a distinct and positive effect – consider the traditional ball-shaped Bays placed outside restaurants. The presence of a topiary plant says 'creative endeavour' and indicates cherished care, its completed features signal reliability, and any novelty aspect hints at mischievous fun. Both indoors and out, topiary is a conversational focal point and highlights the contrasting soft, natural shapes of other herbs. To these qualities, add aromatic leaves to brush by, pat, stroke, sniff, smile at or otherwise engage with, and you have a winning combination, especially by the front door.

## Creating Shapes

Topiary plants can be worked into formal, eccentric or romantic shapes, either in pots or growing in the ground. Choose from geometric balls, cones, columns, pyramids and spirals, symbolic shapes with personal meaning, and jovial animals or objects. Before starting to create your own topiary, it is worth studying other examples: the proportions of stem length, bulk of greenery and pot size are very important to the overall effect.

Clipping is itself a therapeutic and aromatic task. With small plants like Dwarf Box, shaping begins when the plant has reached its desired height. A wire net of the required shape is placed over the plant and anything growing outside the shape is removed. Box is the most popular for intricate forms, herb garden borders and knots, because it responds well to clipping and its condensed root system does not spread out and interfere with neighbouring plants. Box hedging is expensive

ABOVE: *Topiary Bay and Rosemary globes with a spiral of Box. Secure your works of art firmly to prevent light-fingered admirers from whisking them away.*

because it is slow growing, but it is possible to buy a few starter plants to grow on for cuttings until you have enough plants to start a hedge.

To maintain a topiary shape or hedge, clip twice a year: once in late spring or early summer, after new shoots have formed, and again in late summer, allowing time for subsequent new shoots to ripen before the first frosts. This system means that the plant will be clothed in new shoots for most of the year and will maintain a fresh, lively appearance sometimes lacking in evergreens.

### MAKING A BALL-SHAPED BAY

Begin the training process by cultivating just one central stem, removing lower side branches as the shrub grows. Clipping the ball to shape begins when the plant is 15 cm (6 in) taller than the required height, so that the central growing tip can be cut back to encourage the side branches to produce a denser sphere. Trim the side shoots in the sphere to 2–3 leaves. When they have formed 4–5 leaves, clip back again to 2–3 leaves and repeat until the ball shape is achieved. Thereafter, prune with secateurs in early and late summer to maintain the shape, and remove suckers as they appear.

In cold areas, Bay must be grown in pots and taken in under protection for winter, especially in the early years. In borderline climates, use agricultural fleece to protect young plants from frosts, but do not give up on brown-leaved specimens which appear to have been killed – wait for warm weather, and if there was a good root system below the frost level, new shoots will sprout. On the second attempt, leave 7–9 stems up to the ball shape, as this helps to protect against frost damage.

### QUICK SCENTED SHAPES

Other shaped specimens can be created more quickly, using wire frames or hazel wigwams to support plants of Honeysuckle, Akebia, Jasmine, Wisteria or Roses. To train an umbrella-shaped standard, encourage a strong single stem to the desired height, then train stems over an upturned hanging basket for 2 years to give a good shape, and enjoy the aromatic strands wafting in the breeze.

Creative topiary in the famous Villandry garden highlights bright Cosmos flowers (above)
and illustrates contrasting textures of Box and Lavender (below)

# Creating a Potager

A potager is a garden planted with a decorative and useful mix of herbs, vegetables and fruit. To create one in a small town garden, raised beds offer a controllable, tidy, easy-to-maintain-and-harvest solution that is remarkably productive in a small space.

Decide on a few special vegetables such as dwarf Beans, Courgettes and Ruby Chard that taste infinitely better straight from the garden. Choose a fruit such as Fig, Grape, Apple, Pear, Cherry or Peach that can be espaliered or grown horizontally along a fence or on an arch over the path. Then select your favourite herbs and edible flowers, concentrating on variegated, purple and gold forms for extra visual interest. Consider which you need in bulk, such as Chives and Parsley, and those for which a single plant would be sufficient, like Sage.

Possible edging herbs include evergreen dwarf Box, Lavender 'Hidcote', Curry Plant, upright Wall Germander, Alpine Strawberry and Golden Feverfew; herbaceous Chives and Winter Marjoram; biennial Parsley; and colourful annual Calendula, Tagetes and Nasturtium. Give Basil a sunny, protected site where you can keep an eye open for the myriad small insects, snails, birds and larger creatures that share our delight in its flavour.

Remember to keep the centre of each bed a reachable distance, which is about 75 cm (2 ft 6 in) creating a bed 150 cm (5 ft) across, and paths wide enough for a wheelbarrow. In small areas hard paths are preferred to grass as it can be difficult to get a mower into the space. Before planting ensure the soil is absolutely weed-free and enriched with compost. This will allow crops to be planted closer than in a normal garden. By raising the beds a few inches and enclosing them, you will improve the drainage and the plants will be easier to crop.

LEFT: *A potager in spring. Neatly clipped edging creates strong visual interest throughout winter months and provides both contrast and restraint to vigorous summer growth.*

# Small Potager Plan

The design on the opposite page is for a small potager for town or country. It displays the patterns of a potager both as a decorative setting for outdoor entertaining and as the freshest possible source of gourmet vegetables and fruit. Guests can enjoy a garden stroll and select their favourite edible flower or try a new unusual herb garnish.

Formal edgings of Lavender, Dwarf Box and Curry Plant provide a year round design element while the standard-grown ball Bay and wigwams of Climbing Beans and Sweet Peas add height to the visual interest.

## Salad garden

The mini salad potager of 'cut-and-come-again' crops is grown in a movable sink or trough for convenient use and to catch the sun. For 'cut-and-come-again' crops, sow a carpet of seeds in fertile soil. Grow to around 15 cm (6 in) tall, removing any dead leaves and then crop with scissors or sharp knife to 5 cm (2 in). Use the tasty tender leaves in salads, soups, sandwiches, casseroles and as garnish. If kept well watered and fertilized, crops can be harvested three to five times. Experiment with seedling crops of other salad herbs such as Fennel, Orach and Lemon Balm.

# List of Plants in Plan

## Terrace

1. Mini Salad Potager containing surround edging of clipped Chives; 'V' shape dividers of Oak Leaf Lettuce, one purple; one green; 'Cut-and-Come-Again' pattern in-fills: Mustard (*Brassica* spp), Cress (*Lepidium sativum*), Salad Rocket, Fenugreek (*Trigonella foenum-graecum*); Chop Suey Greens (Edible Chrysanthemum); Summer Purslane (*Portulacae oleracea*); Winter Purslane (*Montia perfoliata*)
2. Lemon Verbena
3. Mints (Moroccan Spearmint, Black Peppermint)

4. Climbing Speckled
French (Snap) Bean
'Tongue of Fire' (red
streaked pods)
5. Claret-leaved Grape
('Teinturier' or 'Miller's
Burgundy')
6. Sage
7. Prostrate Rosemary
8. Golden Lemon Thyme

## Potager Garden

9. Espaliered Apple
(scented flowers also
edible)
10. Espaliered Pear
11. Akebia
12. Lavender 'Hidcote'
13. Chives
14. Tarragon
15. Dwarf French Beans
'Purple Tepee'
16. Dwarf Box
17. Calendula
18. Carrot 'Early Nantes'
19. Parsley Curled
20. Purple Basil
21. Madonna Lily
22. Bergamot
23. Rose 'Evelyn'
24. Nasturtium 'Alaska'
25. Ruby Chard
26. Borage
27. Curry Plant
28. Marjoram
29. Bay
30. Sugar Snap Pea
31. Coriander
32. Fan-trained Cherry
'Morello'
33. Dill
34. Runner Bean 'Polestar'
(to attract hummingbirds)
35. Sweet Corn 'Little
Jewels' (purple husks)
36. Courgettes 'Clarella'
37. Squash 'Patti Pan'
37. Sweet Peas
38. Fan-trained Peach

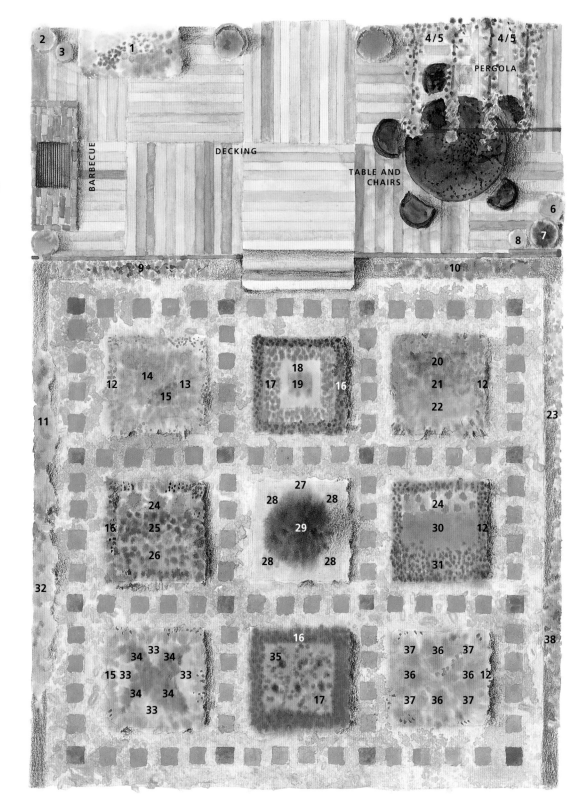

57

# A Potager of Seasonal Herbs

Growing herbs in attractive and convenient beds is not only useful to the entertaining cook, who can pick that vital extra sprig as needed, but also provides an enjoyable background setting for outdoor dining. Here, guests can stroll among the beds and select an unusual garnish, try a new edible flower or experiment with a novel salad ingredient.

This activity also realigns us with seasonal crops. Cooks and gourmets worldwide would agree with the Italian garden proverb 'Everything is good in its season', and value highly the intense flavour of home-grown strawberries in early summer, the first new potatoes with fresh Mint or Dill, garden-fresh courgettes, baby carrots and peas with melted butter and Chives or Tarragon, and thin-skinned, sweet tomatoes ripening alongside lush Basil leaves. Each is enjoyed as it reaches its flavour peak.

# Designing your Garden

## Initial Tasks

- Research herb catalogues and books noting growing conditions.
- Choose your site, ideally with three-quarters in sun.
- Explore the site noting water-logged or windy areas, buried rubble and plants to be kept.
- Consider privacy and note undesirable views.
- Test soil pH levels with a kit.
- Make a tentative list of herbs to grow, noting size, sun and soil needs.

## Preparing the Site

- Clear any weeds.
- Level the area, especially for a knot garden.
- Correct drainage and major soil pH imbalances. Incorporate enriching compost.
- Allow the site to settle over winter for spring planting.

## Measuring the Site on Paper

- Use squared paper, with each square representing say 10 cm or 6 in of your garden space. Indicate the position of North on the paper.
- Measure the site carefully from a base line – a straight path or house wall.
- Mark ground irregularities and large nearby features (trees, gates, sheds, doors and windows) with their shade effect.
- Draw the site neatly in ink and lay transparent paper over it to sketch your design.

## Creating the Design

- Consider enclosure: a hedge width will be 0.66 m (2 ft) or more.
- Choose a formal geometric or informal freeform style considering house architecture.
- Create a pattern of straight, curved or diagonal lines taking inspiration from botanical or decorative geometric patterns.
- Extend lines from existing features onto your plan to see if any of these lines can be incorporated. This integrates the design with existing landscape and architecture.
- Expect to sketch and discard many ideas to establish an overall feel before considering details. Your natural sense of beauty will know when it feels right.
- Translate the lines of your design into paths, beds, steps, arches, seats, or a change of colour or material.
- Avoid a main path rushing straight through the centre of your herb garden; interrupt it with a change of direction or a focal point.
- To test overall balance look at the design in a mirror.
- Consider themed beds e.g. salad herbs or a meditative corner.
- Readjust lines for practicalities – make paths wide enough for a wheel-barrow, allow foot space in front of a seat.
- Incorporate focal points.
- Position verticals or hanging baskets to hide unsightly views.
- Check there are herbs to tantalize all your senses, and to create the mood you wish.

## Placing the Plants

- From your original list, pick your important herbs and give them prime position for access and growing conditions.
- Position the others according to sun requirements with aromatics by paths and seats.

## Marking the Site & Completing the Garden

- Mark the boundary with pegs and string and the design with lime dust or sand trickled from a bag through a small hole.
- Use a large cardboard box as a set square, a cane and a marker on a taut string for circles, and a cardboard template for small repeated shapes.
- Check the final layout. This is the time for adjustments.
- Lay the paths.
- Construct the 'hard' features (arbours, fences, seats).
- Plant the herbs. Most are easy to transplant, so experiment.

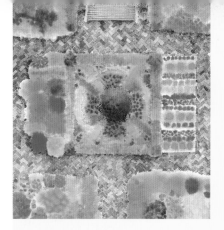

# MOOD GARDENS

*Gardens can be designed to enhance a chosen theme by growing, in accessible places, herbs whose scents are conducive to the desired mood. The atmosphere is developed by choosing sympathetic colours of plants and garden structures, and by combining them with herb species and objects selected to tantalize our other senses. The following designs demonstrate a range of possible atmospheric moods, from refreshing or relaxing to romantic or contemplative. They provide spaces in which to cherish private moments or to share time with friends. But perhaps their most important potential is that through each atmospheric mood created, the gardens offer an opportunity to re-establish our links with Nature and expand our awareness, which is the groundwork for discovering new possibilities and new directions.*

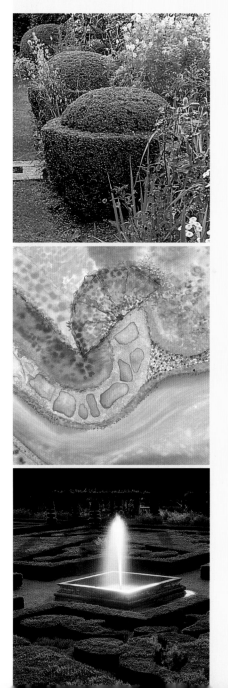

## List of Plants in Plan

1. Dwarf Box
2. Golden Lemon Balm
3. White Musk Mallow
4. Primrose
5. Calendula
6. Sunflower
7. Green Fennel
8. Variegated Ginger Mint
9. Corsican Mint
10. Lawn Chamomile
11. Golden Feverfew
12. Pennyroyal
13. Climbing Rose 'Gloire de Dijon' (yellow-apricot)
14. Climbing Rose 'Mme. Alfred Carrière' (white)
15. Variegated Apple Mint
16. Alecost
17. Cowslip
18. Pots of Lemon Verbena
19. Espaliered Apple tree: 'Worcester Pearmain' – attractive in flower and fruit, and does well in cooler climates, or Crabapples: 'Dartmouth' or 'Montreal' for scented flowers and fruits for delicious preserves.
20. Climbing Nasturtiums

# A Garden of Refreshing Morning Plants

A delightful way to start the day is to breakfast in a bright refreshing garden space. This simple design, suitable for town or country, is enriched with decorative pebble path patterns and a mosaic of jewel-like pool tiles. The invigorating Mint, Lemon and Apple scents are amplified by bright gold and green leaves, butter-yellow Primrose, golden-orange Calendula and the embodiment of sunshine – the tall friendly Sunflower (*Helianthus annus*). The morning brightness is reflected in the white Musk Mallow (*Malva moschata alba*), which flowers continuously all summer. Classical screens of vertical bamboo add to the feeling of lightness, provide privacy and complement the sparkling light and refreshing sound of the miniature tumble of water along the water channel.

Design with clean lines and open spaces to encourage a sense of clarity, and plant easy-maintenance herbs in simple shapes – restrict intricate patterns. Then take deep exhilarating breaths and enjoy the new day.

BELOW: *The golden shrub foliage, white flowers and neatly clipped topiary offer a stimulating space for a morning walk.*

# *Relaxing Rainbow Healing Garden*

The plan for this aromatherapy garden is an eight-petalled 'flower' with one 'petal' acting as the entrance and space for outdoor massage, and the other seven as mini gardens. There is a central seating area around an almond tree that allows a view of each segment. Each contains one or more aromatherapy plants plus others of the relevant colour. Plant tall plants on the outer edges, grading to smallest plants near the apex.

## *Suggested Plants*

### *Code*

**A** Plants which yield essential oils or pressed oils.
**B** Other aromatic plants with appropriate flower or leaf colour.
**C** Healing herbs and others with appropriate flower and leaf colour.

### *Red*
(SCARLET TO PINK)

**A** Old Roses: 'Guinée', 'Mme Isaac Pereire', 'Souvenir du Docteur Jamain', 'Empereur du Maroc', 'Prince Charles', 'Duke of Wellington'; Rose Geraniums; scarlet Clove Pinks; Honeysuckle *repens*; Lavender 'Hidcote Pink'.
**B** Magnolia Vine (*Schisandra chinensis*); Soapwort; Bergamot; scarlet Peony; pink Musk mallow; pink Hyacinth. In warmer climates California Allspice (*Calycanthus occidentalis*).
**C** red Opium or Field Poppies; Crimson Clover

(*Trifolium incarnatum*); red Lupin; Wall Germander; Lady's Smock (*Cardamine pratensis*); Gay Feather (*Liatris spicata*); Wood Betony (*Stachys officinalis*).

### *Orange*
(WARM GOLDEN ORANGES)

**A** Rose 'Elizabeth of Glamis'; Rose 'Alchemist', 'Sweet Magic', 'Geraldine', 'Heaven Scent', 'Southampton'.
**B** Honeysuckle (*L. x tellmanniana*); climbing Nasturtiums; *Buddleia globosa*; *Lilium henryi*; Madonna Lily; Edible Chrysanthemum; Mignonette; Tagetes 'Tangerine Gem'; Nasturtium; Wild Wallflower (*Cheiranthus cheiri*); Peony 'Souvenir de Maxime Cornu'.
**C** California Poppy (*Eschscholzia californica*); Calendula.

### *Yellow*
(SUNNY BUTTER YELLOWS AND YELLOW-SPLASHED LEAVES)

**A** golden Hop; Evening

Primrose; Gold variegated Lemon Balm; golden Lemon Thyme; Chamomiles: yellow Jasmine (*Jasminum humile*); Incense Rose (*R. primula*), Rose 'Canary Bird', 'Fresia', 'Leverkusen', 'Cloth of Gold'.
**B** Japanese Honeysuckle; Ginger Mint; yellow Narcissus and Jonquils; Mignonette; golden Feverfew; variegated Apple Mint; Melilot; Agrimony; Tansy; *Paeonia lutea*; Elecampane (*Inula helenium*).
**C** Sunflowers; Foxglove (*Digitalis lutea*); Giant Cowslip (*Primula florindae*); Winter Jasmine (*Jasminum nudiflorum*); Lady's Mantle; Dyer's Chamomile; Mullein; Golden Rod (*Solidago virgaurea*); *Iris pseudacorus*; Arnica.

### *Green*
(GREEN AND WHITE FOLIAGE AND FLOWERS)

**A** Fennel; Peppermint; Lemon Balm; Geranium; *Lavandula viridis*; Sweet Marjoram; Mints; Basil; Rosemary; Thymes; Sweet Myrtle; Angelica; Hops.
**B** Dang Shen (*Codonopsis pilosula*); Sweet Cicely; Tobacco Plant (*Nicotiana alata* 'Lime Green'); Sweet Woodruff; Parsley; Corsican Mint; Lawn Chamomile 'Treneague'; Pennyroyal; Chervil; Solomon's Seal.
**C** Yam (*Dioscorea discolor*); Ivy 'Parsley Crested'.

### *Blue*
(GREEN AND BLUE FOLIAGE AND LIGHT BLUE FLOWERS)

**A** Borage; Rosemary; prostrate Sage; Lavender 'Munstead'; Flax.

**B** *Crocus thomasinianus*.
**C** *Clematis alpina* 'Frances Rivis'; *Convolvulus* 'Heavenly Blue'; *Lobelia syphilitica*; *Camassia quamash*; Bluebell; Forget-Me-Not; Scilla; Harebell; Flax; Virginia Skullcap; Soft/Blue Comfrey (*Symphytum asperum*); Love-in-a-Mist; Periwinkle (*Vinca major*); Jacob's Ladder (*Polemonium caeruleum*); Phacelia; Lungwort; Cornflower (*Centaurea cyanus*), Sea Holly (*Eryngium maritimum*); Rue 'Jackman's Blue'; Iris 'Mary Frances'.

### *Indigo*
(DARK BLUE FLOWERS AND GREEN FOLIAGE)

**A** Rock Hyssop; Dark blue Lavender ('Folgate', 'Twickle' or 'Sawyers' Selection');
**B** Catnip.
**C** Clematis 'Jackmanii Superba'; Wisteria 'Violaceo-plena'; Monkshood (*Aconitum napellus*); dark blue Delphiniums; *Lobelia syphilitica*; *Scilla siberica*; *Ajuga reptans* 'Atropurpurea'; Self Heal (*Prunella vulgaris*); Larkspur (*Consolida ambigua*); Alkanet (*Anchusa officinalis*); Balloon Flower (*Platycodon grandiflorum*); Iris 'Matinata'.

### *Violet*
(VIOLET AND PURPLE FLOWERS; GREEN AND PURPLE LEAVES)

**A** bronze Fennel; Clary Sage; Eau-de-Cologne Mint; purple Sage; purple-leaf Basil; Sweet Violets; Lavender 'Hidcote' and *L. stoechas*; dark-leaved Mints.
**B** Akebia; purple Sweet Peas; Anise Hyssop; Saffron

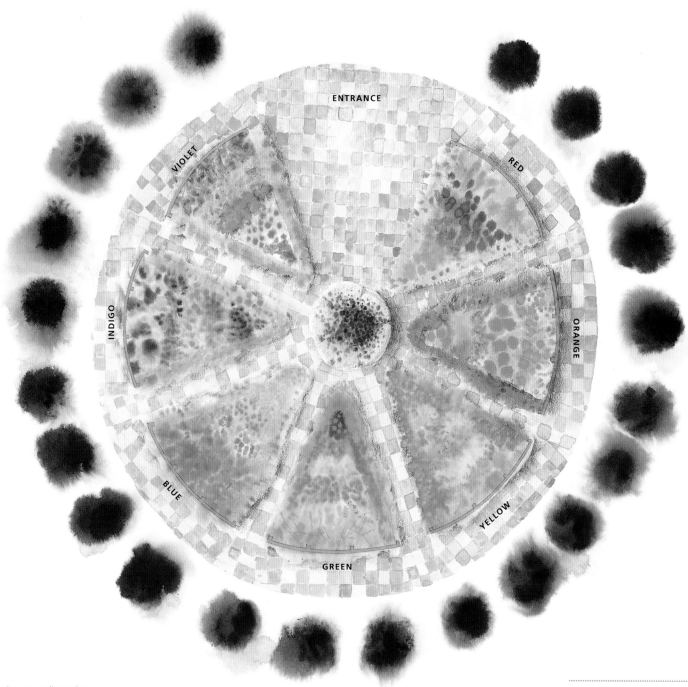

Crocus; *Heliotropium arborescens*; Lilac; Buddleia; Sweet Rocket; Catmint; Honeysuckle var. *repens*. **C** purple-leaf Grape 'Teinturier'; Milk Thistle (*Silybum marianum*); Scotch Thistle (*Onopordum acanthium*); *Echinacea*; purple Orach; purple Plantain; Globe artichoke; purple-leaf Hazel; violet Passion flower; dark purple Hollyhock (*Alcea rosea*); purple Columbine; purple Penstemon; Iris 'Paradise Bird'.

ABOVE: *This garden is made up of seven segments, to represent either the seven days of the week, the seven major chakras or the seven colours of the rainbow.*

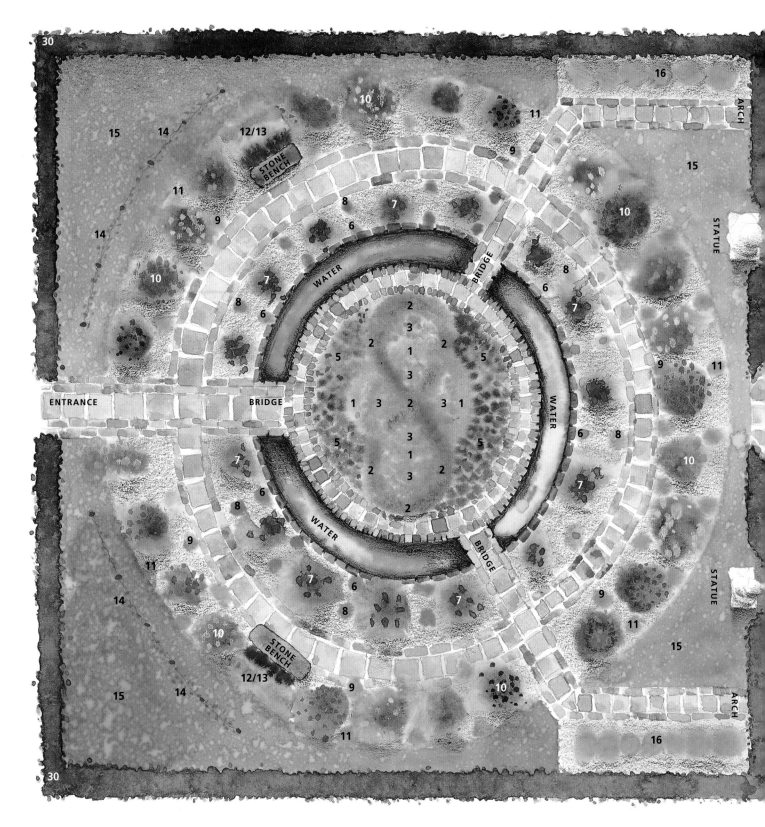

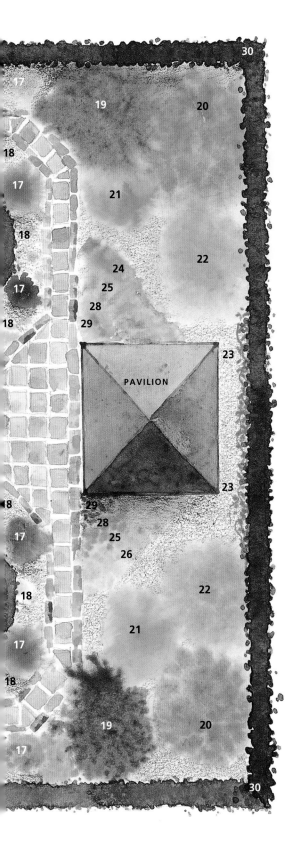

# Secret Garden

Fragrant flowers speak to us directly. The fragile petals, luminous colour and delicate scent can convey subtle emotions more eloquently than words, making them universal symbols of love. With the wealth of associations between plants and romance, the secret garden has evolved as a place for lovers to meet out of public gaze. In this garden the private fragrant space is hidden, waiting to be discovered amid the tall curved Yew hedges with mysterious areas of light and dark, and the occasional waft of sweet fragrance to enhance the sense of expectation.

ABOVE: *A narrow arch through the Yew hedge beckons to a secret garden.*

## List of Plants in Plan

### Lover's Knot (centre)
1. Silver Santolina (*Santolina chamaecyparissus* syn *S. incana*)
2. Box
3. Sweet Violet
4. Miniature Roses in scarlet, pink and white
5. Clove Pinks

### First Ring
6. Iris, smoky blues and violets
7. Peony, scented in scarlet, pink and white
8. Gypsophila, white

### Second Ring
9. Geranium 'Johnson's Blue'
10. 'Old' Shrub Roses in scarlets, pinks and whites
11. Delphinium, deep blue
12. Bergamot, scarlet flowers
13. Madonna Lilies, white

### Surround
14. Climbing Roses
15. Lawn
16. Southernwood (next to path leading to secret area)

### Secret Garden
17. Sweet Cicely
18. Eau-de-Cologne Mint
19. Buddleia, scented purple flowers
20. Lilac, lilac to blue flowers
21. Osmanthus, scented white flowers and dark evergreen leaves

22. Philadelphus, white flowers
23. Purple Honeysuckle (*Lonicera japonica* var. *repens*), purple-red stems and purple-pink flowers
24. Soapwort, double pink flowers
25. Sweet William (*Dianthus barbatus*)
26. White Evening Primrose
27. Sweet Rocket, lilac and white forms
28. Narcissus, white ('Cheerfulness')
29. Thyme 'Fragrantissimus'

### Hedging
30. Yew

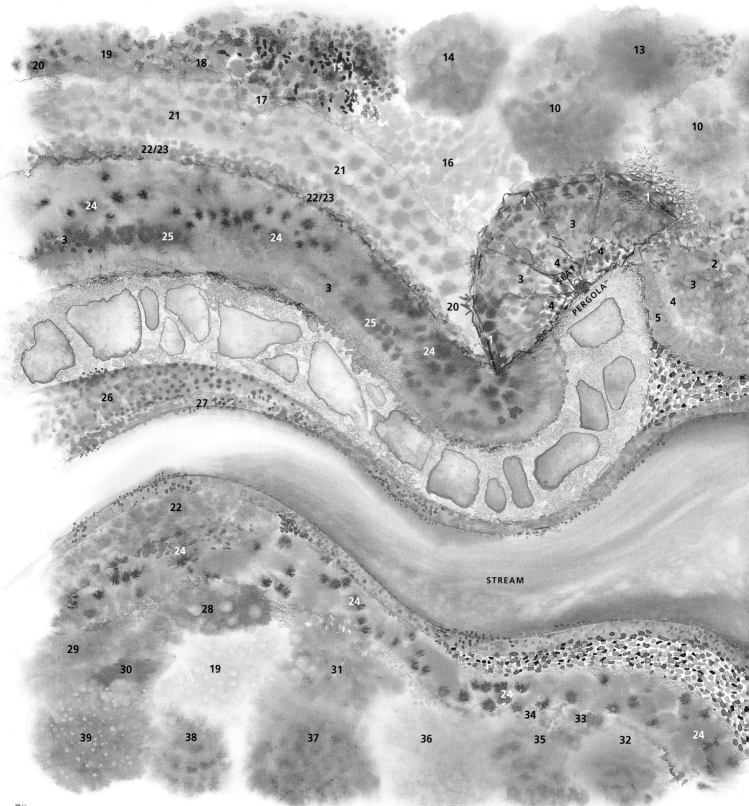

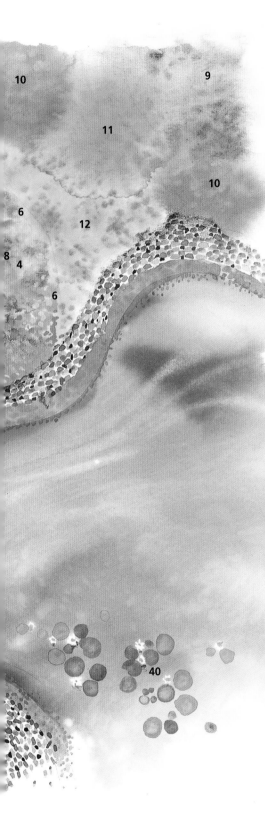

## List of Plants in Plan

### Pergola Area

1. Wisteria, white and purple
2. Night-Scented Stocks (*Mathiola longipetala* subsp. *bicornis*)
3. Sweet Violet
4. Lily-of-the-Valley
5. Silver Artemisia (*A. schmidtiana* 'Nana')
6. Purple Honeysuckle var. 'repens'
7. Camassia
8. Sweet Woodruff

### Main Area

9. Linden Tree
10. Silver Birch
11. White Bramble (*Rubus biflorus* var. *quinqueflorus*)
12. Bluebells
13. Cut-leaf Elder
14. Winter-flowering Honeysuckle (*Lonicera* x *purpusii*)
15. Delphinium, deep blue
16. Peony, white
17. Purple Sage
18. Southernwood
19. White Evening Primrose
20. Borage
21. Silver Santolina
22. Catmint
23. Chamomile
24. Lavender 'Hidcote'
25. Purple Petunia
26. Thyme 'Fragrantissimus'
27. Moss
28. Madonna Lily
29. Clary Sage
30. Anise Hyssop
31. Sweet Rocket
32. Meadowsweet
33. Sweet Cicely
34. Monkshood (*Aconitum napellus*)
35. Buddleia, blue
36. Tree Poppy (*Romneya coulteri*)
37. Lilac, purple
38. Angelica
39. Philadelphus
40. White Water Lily (*Nymphaea* 'Gonnère')

# Night-Scented Nightingale Garden

As light fades into evening, sounds, textures and fragrance are heightened. Among the crickets and cicadas, frogs and owls, the most hauntingly beautiful sound must be that of the nightingale. Legend tells of the love between a nightingale and a Lily-of-the-Valley, and how the bird would not return to the wood until the flower bloomed each spring. In this garden Lily-of-the-Valley and Bluebells are planted in the woods amidst an undergrowth of Nettles and Bramble to entice the nightingale to nest there. The white trunks of Birch trees and the sensuous curves of silver, white and blue plants all shimmer in the starlight. The timber frame provides an arbour for fragrant Wisteria. The perfume of Honeysuckle, Sweet Rocket and Night-Scented Stock are strongest in the evening, and twilight triggers the opening of Evening Primrose to release its honey scent and faint luminescence. The fragrances of Lilac, Philadelphus and Buddleia waft on the evening breeze and, with the rich purple, blues and iridescent whites, create a velvety cloak of serenity and peace.

# Moonlight Meditation Garden

To be in the presence of a sacred grove of noble trees touches a memory of ancient wisdom. Within this ring of thirteen Druid calendar trees is a circle of Silver Sagebrush; the inner circles of calming white Lavender and silver Thyme complete the peaceful atmosphere and allow thoughts to soar to the starry night sky. Then a waft of aromatic herbs gently reconnects us to the earth.

A fragrant grove could also be created with a surround of the Incense Cedar (*Calocedrus decurrens*) which has powerfully scented wood and foliage, or the Juniper tree with its protective aromatic needles. Below the trees grow Sweet Grass for its new-mown hay scent and to burn in purification ceremonies following the natives of North America. Lawn Chamomile underfoot means every movement will release sweet fragrance.

In the centre of this reflective space, make a moon dial to trace the path of the moon or place a shallow bowl of water to reflect it. Float perfumed flowers or scented candles in the bowl for a magical evening. And after a time in the peaceful serenity of this meditation garden, retire to tranquil slumber.

ABOVE: *The play of evening light and water creates a magical atmosphere in a formal garden of clipped herbs.*

## List of Plants in Plan

### Trees
1. Birch
2. Rowan
3. Ash
4. Alder
5. Willow
6. Hawthorn
7. Oak
8. Holly
9. Hazel
10. Vine (on post)
11. Ivy (on post)
12. Dwarf Elder
13. Elder

### Underplanting
14. White Bluebells (*Hyacinthoides hispanica* 'La Grandesse')
15. Sweetgrass

### Inner Circle
16. Sagebrush
17. White Evening Primrose
18. Madonna Lily
19. Moonflower (*Ipomoea alba*)
20. Lavender, white
21. Narcissus, white
22. Pinks, white 'Mrs Sinkins'
23. Chamomile
24. Silver Thyme

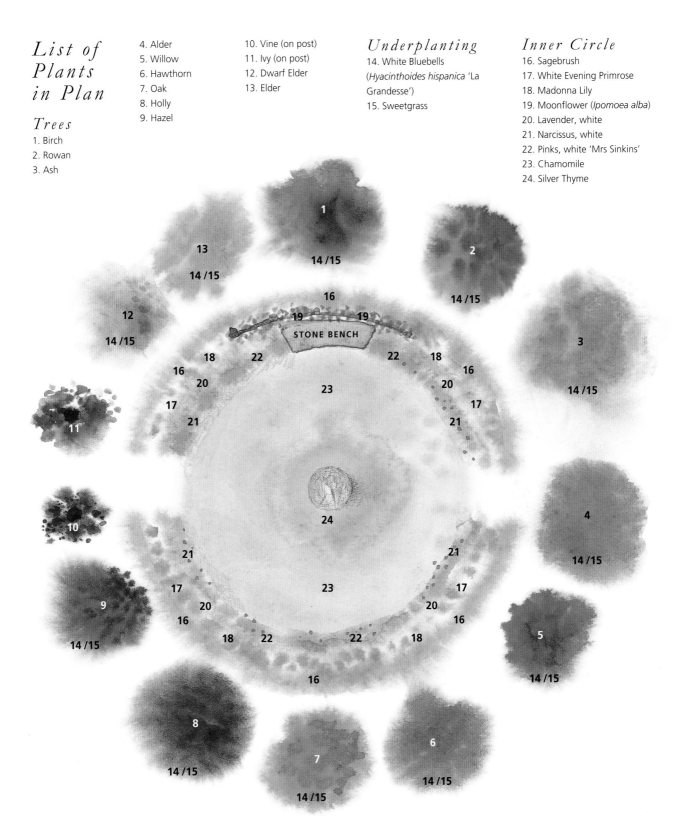

# Cultivation & Harvesting

The plants are listed alphabetically by their Latin botanical name with the common name also indicated. The zoning system (Z1–11) states average annual minimum temperature but must be regarded only as a rough indication as many other factors affect whether or not a plant will thrive: these include humidity, summer temperature, wind factor, soil type, annual rainfall, drainage, genetic plant characteristics and so on. Similar factors also affect the height and spread that a particular specimen will reach at maturity, but a guide is given for each plant.

*H = height, S = spread.*

## Average annual minimum temperature zones

| Zone | °F | °C |
|------|------|------|
| 1 | below -50 | below -45.5 |
| 2 | -50 to -40 | -45.5 to -40.1 |
| 3 | -40 to -30 | -40.0 to -34.5 |
| 4 | -30 to -20 | -34.4 to -28.9 |
| 5 | -20 to -10 | -28.8 to -23.4 |
| 6 | -10 to 0 | -23.3 to -17.8 |
| 7 | 0 to 10 | -17.7 to -12.3 |
| 8 | 10 to 20 | -12.2 to -6.7 |
| 9 | 20 to 30 | -6.6 to -1.2 |
| 10 | 30 to 40 | -1.1 to 4.4 |
| 11 | above 40 | above 4.4 |

*Agastache foeniculum*
ANISE HYSSOP
Perennial or biennial with aniseed scented leaves and mauve flowers.
*Z 8; H 80cm (32in); S 45cm (18in).*
Plant in sun in rich, moist, well-drained soil. Anise Hyssop and mint-scented Korean Mint (*A. rugosa*) cross-pollinate, making identification difficult – use leaf scent as a guide. *A. mexicana* has eucalyptus scented leaves. Sow seed in spring; divide creeping roots in summer. Dry leaves and stems in summer.

*Akebia quinata*
AKEBIA
Semi-evergreen climber with pendulous purple, honey-vanilla-scented flowers and occasionally sausage-shaped edible fruits.
*Z 5; H 12m (40ft); S 6m (20ft).*
Plant in sun or semi-shade in moisture-retentive, well-drained soil. Sow seed in spring, take semi-ripe cuttings in summer with bottom heat or layer in winter. Protect young plants in winter. Dislikes being moved.

*Allium* species
ALLIUMS
Bulbous perennials or biennials including chive, garlic and onion.
*Z 4–9; H to 1m (3ft); S to 30cm (1ft).*
Most are frost hardy. Grow in sun or part shade in rich, moist, well-drained soil. Take offsets or divide bulbs in autumn or spring; plant Garlic cloves 4cm (1½in) deep in autumn. Sow seed in spring. Thin to 23cm (9in); Garlic to 15cm (6in). Water in dry spells and enrich the soil annually (or monthly, when cutting Chives). Divide and replant clumps every 3–4 years. Pot up in autumn for an indoor supply.

*Aloysia triphylla*
(syn. *Lippia citriodora*)
LEMON VERBENA
Shrub with long-lasting, lemon-scented leaves and white or pale purple flowers.
*Z 8; H 3m (10ft); S 2m (6ft).*
Half hardy. Only plant outdoors in a well-drained, sunny, sheltered spot if winter temperature does not drop below –10ºC (14ºF). New growth can appear very late so never discard a plant until late summer. A conservatory, greenhouse or pot plant enjoys being outdoors in summer, indoors in winter. Prune lax stems for shape and again in autumn. Take softwood cuttings in late spring or sow seed in spring. Use fresh, and dry for winter use.

*Anethum graveolens*
DILL
Annual with uniquely flavoured foliage, yellow flowerheads and oval seeds.
*Z 8; H 1m (3ft); S 30cm (12in).*
Frost hardy. Grow in full sun in a sheltered position in rich, well-drained soil. Dill prefers the long days of northern climates. Do not plant near Fennel, as the two cross-pollinate and flavours become muddled. Sow *in situ* from spring until midsummer. Seeds are viable for 3–10 years. Self-seeds. Thin to 23–30cm (9–12in) apart. Can be grown indoors. Gather the leaves when young. Pick flowering tops just as fruits begin to form and infuse them in vinegar. To collect seed after the flowering heads turn brown, hang the whole plant over a cloth.

*Angelica archangelica*
ANGELICA
3-year 'biennial' with large juniper/gin-scented leaves and 13cm (6in) greenish-white spherical flowerheads.
*Z 4; H 3m (10ft); S 1.3m (4½ft).*
Grow in lightshade in deep, moist soil. Allow the plants to self-seed or sow in early autumn with fresh seed.

*Anthriscus cerefolium*
CHERVIL
Culinary annual with fern-like aniseed-parsley-flavoured, finely divided leaves.
*Z 6; H 60cm (24in); S 30cm (12in).*
Grow in fertile, light soil, in partial shade in summer as it quickly runs to seed in hot sun. Autumn seedlings enjoy full winter sun. Ripe seed germinates quickly and can be used 6 – 8 weeks after sowing. Scatter on the soil and press in lightly. Thin seedlings to 20cm (8in) apart. Chervil does not transplant well. In winter, give cloche protection against hungry creatures. Pick when above 10cm (4in) tall. Left to self-seed, Chervil will give a spring and autumn crop.

*Artemisia dracunculus*
TARRAGON, FRENCH
Perennial with sweet, peppery, aniseed-scented leaves and tiny flowers.
*Z 3; H 1m (3ft); S 40cm (16in).*
Half hardy. Grow in a sunny, sheltered position in light, dryish, humus-rich soil. Divide roots in spring; take stem cuttings in summer. Thin or transplant to 30–45cm (12–18in). Cut back in autumn. Give winter protection of straw or mulch. Can be grown indoors. Harvest healthy leaves and freeze or dry at 27ºC (80ºF), or infuse in oil or vinegar.

*Artemisia* species
ARTEMISIAS
Group of herbs with pungent silver foliage and insignificant flowers.
*Z 3–8; H 9cm–2.5m (3½in–8ft); S 30cm–1.4m (12in–4½ft).*
Full sun in light, dry, well-drained soil. Site carefully as rain washes growth-inhibiting toxin out of the leaves, affecting nearby plants. Sow seed when available. Take semi-hardwood cuttings in late summer. Divide every 3–4 years.

*Borage officinalis*
BORAGE
Hardy culinary annual with rough-textured cucumber-scented leaves and sky blue star flowers.
*Z 7; H 1m (3ft); S 60cm (24in).*
Prefers open, sunny position in light, dry, well-drained soil. Sow seed *in situ* or singly in pots in spring for summer flowers; autumn for spring flowers. Self-seeds freely. Set young plants 30cm (12in) apart. Can appear messy when it grows large. Plant specimens among pink roses for support and a mutual colour intensifying effect.

*Calendula officinalis*
CALENDULA/POT MARIGOLD
A culinary and medicinal annual with golden-orange daisy-like flowers. The whole plant has a sharp clean scent.
*Z 6; H & S 70cm (28in).*
Grow in a sunny position, preferably in fine loam, although it tolerates most except waterlogged soils. Sow seed in spring *in situ* or singly in pots. Plant 30–45cm (12–18in) apart. Deadhead for continuous flowers.

*Chamaemelum nobile* (Roman)
and *Matricaria recutita* (German)
CHAMOMILE
Roman, evergreen perennial, has apple-scented leaves and sports two forms: double-flowered and non-flowering (*C. n.* 'Treneague'). German, or annual, has non-scented leaves. Both have feathery foliage and yellow-centred white daisy flowers with an earthy-scent.
*Z 4; H 15–40cm (6–15in); S 45cm (18in).*
Grow in full sun, in light, well-drained soil. Sow seed in spring. Divide perennials in spring or autumn. Take 8cm (3in) cuttings from side shoots in summer. For a lawn or seat of Chamomile, plant 10–15cm (4–6in) apart. Plant annuals 23cm (9in) apart. Pick leaves any time. Pick fully open flowers, dry and store in airtight, lightproof containers.

*Cistus ladanifer*
LABDANUM
Evergreen shrub exudes sticky balsamic resin with leaden appearance. The large white-petalled flowers have a crimson spot.
*Z 7; H & S 2.5m (8ft).*
Grow in full sun in well-drained, light to poor soil. Sow seed in autumn or spring, and take softwood cuttings in late summer. Remove damaged twigs and dead flowers in spring, but avoid hard pruning. Dislikes disturbance.

*Citrus* species
CITRUS
16 evergreen trees and shrubs with perfumed flowers and aromatic fruit.
*Z 7–9; H 10m (30ft); S 7m (22ft).*
Tender trees. Grow in deep, well-drained but moisture-retentive loam. In temperate climates, Oranges, Lemons and Grapefruit can be grown outside during the summer, and brought into a cool, light room before the first frosts. Lemon is easiest to grow, Grapefruit the largest. Pummelo (*C. maxima*), Meyer Lemon (*C. meyeri*), Lemon (*C. limon*) and Seville orange (*C. aurantium*) are suitable for large pot cultivation. Pots should be terracotta or have aeration holes

drilled in the sides. Under glass, mist daily and keep well ventilated during summer. When watering, soak the plant well, then leave until almost completely dry before watering again. In winter, plants may need watering only once every 10 weeks (too much hinders flowering); increase this from spring onwards, and feed regularly when in full growth. When plants bloom indoors, ensure a good crop-set by touching each flower with a dry camel's-hair brush dipped in pollen. Oranges and Lemons take up to a year to ripen, which can result in fragrant flowers at the same time as colourful fruits. Air- or oven-dry peel and store in an airtight tub.

*Comptonia peregrina*
SWEET FERN
Low shrub with spicy fern-like leaves.
*Z 4; H 1.5m (5ft); S 1.2m (4ft).*
Grow in sun or partial shade in well-drained acid soils which remain moist in the growing season. Sow ripe seed and overwinter in a cold frame. Replant rooted suckers in spring. Dislikes being transplanted. Harvest and dry young leaves in early summer.

*Convallaria majalis*
LILY-OF-THE-VALLEY
Perennial with perfumed white, bell-like flowers and a scented rhizome.
*Z 3; H 23cm (9in); S indefinite.*
Grow in dappled shade beneath deciduous trees in humus-rich, moist but well-drained soil. Sow seed in spring. Divide clumps in early autumn, then plant shallowly 15cm (6in) apart. Mice may eat the rhizome.

*Coriandrum sativum*
CORIANDER
Annual with pungent feathery leaves, white to mauve flowers and spicy seeds.
*Z 7; H 50cm (20 in); S 30cm (12in).*
Full sun in light, rich soil. Sow in autumn, to overwinter in mild climates, or early spring in the final position, away from Fennel which suffers in its presence. Thin to 20cm

(8in) apart. Plants run to seed in hot summer weather. 'Cilantro' gives a good leaf crop, 'Morocco' a bumper seed harvest.

*Crocus sativus*
SAFFRON
The mauve flowers of this crocus have protruding stigmas which are picked to become the earthy spice, Saffron.
*Z 6; H 23cm (9in); S 10cm (4in).*
Grow in a sunny, warm position in well-drained, alkaline soil enriched with manure or in pots in a cold greenhouse. Corms increase by producing 'baby' corms, so after 4 years, dig up in late summer, break off new corms and plant them 12cm (5in) deep and apart. They require a long, hot summer to flower. Harvest autumn stigmas in the morning. For a slightly lighter flavour, remove the white base. Wrap loosely in absorbent paper, dry for 2–3 days away from light and damp until brittle, and store in an airtight container.

*Cymbopogon citratus*
LEMON GRASS
Perennial grass with sweet lemon-scented bulbous stems and blade leaves.
*Z 9; H 1.5m (5ft); S 1m (3ft).*
Tender. In temperate areas, grow as a houseplant in a moisture-retentive mix in moderate humidity, min temp 10–13°C (50–55°F). Water regularly. Pot on to avoid crowded roots. Propagate by division. Try growing from grocers' fresh bulbous-based stalks – place in water until roots develop, then plant.

*Eucalyptus* species
EUCALYPTUS
Over 500 species of trees and shrubs with scented leaves, gums and oils.
*Z 10; H 70m (230ft); S 25m (80ft).*
Tender or half hardy. In temperate climates, grow in a sheltered position in well-drained, moist soil with a thick mulch, or as a pot plant brought inside when frosts start. Prune Blue Gums annually or biennially to

maintain attractive juvenile foliage. Keep conservatory specimens in full sun and well ventilated; water moderately when in growth. Common varieties are easy from seed.

*Ferula assafoetida*
ASAFOETIDA
Tall perennial with feathery foliage and umbels of creamy-yellow flowers.
*Z 8; H 2m (6ft); S 1m (3ft).*
Borderline hardy. Grow in a sunny position in deep, moist, well-drained soil. It dislikes being moved. Sow fresh, ripe seed in late summer. The musky-fishy-scented gum is bled from living 5-year-old roots and dried.

*Filipendula ulmaria*
MEADOWSWEET
Tall perennial with wintergreen-scented leaves and frothy, cream, almond-scented summer flowerheads.
*Z 2; H 2m (6ft); S 45cm (18in).*
Sun or partial shade in moist to wet fertile, alkaline soil. Sow in spring; divide in spring or autumn. Thin or transplant to 30cm (12in) apart.

*Foeniculum vulgare*
FENNEL
Tall aniseed-scented perennial, with finely cut green or bronze foliage and umbels of yellow flowers.
*Z 5; H 2m (6ft); S 1m (3ft).*
Full sun in well-drained loam soil; avoid heavy clay. Sow in late spring to early summer. Self-seeds when established. Divide in autumn. Thin or transplant to 50cm (20in). Do not grow near dill as cross-pollinated seed flavours are muddled, or near coriander, which reduces fennel's seed production.

*Fragaria vesca*
WILD STRAWBERRY
Perennial with toothed leaflets faintly scented in autumn and sweet fruit.
*Z 5; H & S 20cm (8in).*
Grow in a cool, sunny or shady position in humus-rich, moist, well-drained alkaline soil. Sow seed in

spring. To avoid the erratic germination caused by the seed's hard shell, sow in heat 18°C (65°F) with high humidity. Transplant daughter plants (produced on runners) to 30cm (12in) apart. Keep well watered. A potash fertilizer is beneficial when fruits begin to set. Pick ripe fruits to encourage more.

*Helichrysum italicum*
CURRY PLANT
Aromatic evergreen curry-scented sub-shrub with intensely silver foliage and mustard yellow flowers.
*Z 8; H & S 50cm (20in).*
Grow in sheltered sunny position in well drained soil. Give protection at –5°C (22°F). Take stem cuttings in spring or autumn.

*Hesperis matronalis*
SWEET ROCKET
Upright biennial, with white to purple, violet-clove-scented flowers.
*Z 3; H 1m (3ft); S 25cm (10in).*
Grow in full sun or light shade in moist, well-drained soil. Tolerates poor soils, but double-flowered forms need more nutrients. Sow *in situ* in autumn or spring; take basal cuttings in spring; divide in autumn or winter. Deadhead to encourage further flowering.

*Humulus lupulus* and *H. l. 'Aureus'*
HOPS
Climber with large, green or gold leaves and beer-scented 'strobiles' (papery bracts on female flowers).
*Z 5; H 7m (21ft); S 6m (18ft).*
Grow female plants in sunny open position in fertile deeply dug soil. Separate rooted stems and suckers in spring. Take cuttings in early summer. Pick ripe strobiles in early autumn. Dry or freeze for immediate use.

*Hyssopus officinalis*
HYSSOP
Semi-evergreen sub-shrub with peppery-green scented leaves and spikes of blue, white or pink aromatic flowers in late

summer. Rock Hyssop (*H.o.subsp aristatus*) is a compact form with purple flowers.
*Z 3; H 1m (3ft); S 90cm (32in).*
Full sun in light, well-drained, alkaline soil. Divide roots in spring. Take stem cuttings from spring to autumn. Sow species in spring. Grow 60cm apart, or 30cm for hedging. Prune after flowering in mild climates; otherwise in spring.

*Iris germanica* var. *florentina*
ORRIS/FLORENTINE IRIS
Perennial with sword-like leaves and white to pale-blue, honey-scented flowers.
*Z 6; H 1m (3ft); S indefinite.*
Grow in a sunny position in well-drained neutral to alkaline soil. Propagate by removing offsets in late summer. Sow seed in autumn. Lift rhizomes in late summer/early autumn to dry for 3 years to produce violet scent. Root is then powdered.

*Jasminum officinale*
JASMINE
Deciduous shrub has 5-petalled white flowers with narcotic perfume.
*Z 7; H 1–10m (3–30ft); S 2–10m (6–30ft).*
Sunny position in rich, well-drained soil. Provide climbing support. Sow seed in spring; take semi-ripe cuttings in summer. Thin out shoots or cut back after flowering.

*Juniperus communis*
JUNIPER
Aromatic tree with needle leaves and gin-scented berries.
*Z 2–7; H 10m (30ft); S 4m (12ft).*
Grow in an exposed, sunny site in moist soil. Both male and female plants are necessary for berry production. To ensure plant gender, cultivate from semi-hardwood cuttings taken from known plants in late summer to early autumn.

*Laurus nobilis*
BAY
Evergreen tree or shrub with thick spicy leaves and small cream flowers.
*Z 8; H 15m (50ft); S 10m (30ft).*

Sheltered site in sun; rich, moist, well-drained soil. Deeply rooted mature plants recover from frost but young plants are killed by freezing winds. Difficult to propagate. Take 10cm (4 in) stem cuttings in late summer in a heated, humid propagator. Bring pot-grown plants indoors if temperature drops below –15°C (5°F). Can be clipped into a ball shape.

*Lavandula* species
LAVENDER
Evergreen sub-shrub has 28 species and many varieties with silvery leaves and spikes of fragrant summer flowers.
*Z 5–9; H 75cm (30in); S 1.2m (4ft).*
Grow in an open, sunny site in well-drained, open, limey soil. Take 10–20cm (4–8in) stem cuttings in autumn or spring, or divide or layer the plant. Sow species from fresh seed in late summer. Thin or transplant to 45–60cm (18–24in) apart. Prune in late autumn or spring. Harvest flowers at maximum opening.

*Levisticum officinale*
LOVAGE
Perennial with beefy-celery-flavoured leaves and umbels of green-yellow flowers.
*Z 4; H 2m (6ft); S 1.5m (5ft).*
Full sun or part shade in rich, moist, well-drained soil. Sow fresh ripe seed in late summer; self-seeds readily. Thin or transplant to 60cm (24in). Tie straw around the stems 2–3 weeks before harvesting for use as a blanched, tender vegetable.

*Lilium candidum*
MADONNA LILY
Bulb produces a rosette of new basal leaves and heavily perfumed white flowers.
*Z 6; H 2m (6ft); S 45cm (18in).*
Plant in early autumn in a sunny, sheltered spot in well-drained alkaline soil, 5cm (2in) below soil level. Do not allow to dry out or disturb the bulbs. Propagate by seed sown in spring or autumn; by 'scales' (outside surface of a large bulb) in summer; or by offsets (mini bulbs) in late summer.

*Lonicera periclymenum*
HONEYSUCKLE
Climbing, twining perennial with intensely perfumed pink and cream flowers.
*Z 4; H 4m (40ft); S Climber.*
Grow in well-drained soil in sun or light shade. Take cuttings from non-flowering shoots in summer and root in sandy compost. Plant out in autumn or winter.

*Melilotus officinalis*
MELILOT
Biennial with spires of honey-vanilla-scented small, yellow flowers in summer.
*Z 3; H 1.2m (4ft); S 1m (3ft).*
Grow in sun or light shade in well-drained soil. Sow in spring or late summer. Self-seeds in light soils. Thin or transplant to 45cm (18in) apart.

*Melissa officinalis*
LEMON BALM
Bushy perennial with green or gold variegated, mildly lemon-scented, scalloped leaves and tiny white flowers.
*Z 4; H 1.2m (4ft); S 1m (3ft).*
Sunny site with midday shade in ordinary, moist soil. Gold leaves scorch in midday sun. Sow in spring; germination is slow. Divide the plant in spring or autumn. Transplant to 60cm (24in). Prune to keep tidy shape.

*Mentha* species
MINTS
Perennials with invasive rootstocks with a variety of leaf scents and flower colours.
*Z 3; H 1.2m (4ft); S indefinite.*
Grow in sun or partial shade in moist, well-drained, nutrient-rich alkaline soil where invasive roots will not be a problem. Divide in spring or autumn. Take cuttings in spring or summer and root in compost or water. Remove flowering stems to avoid cross-pollination between species. If rust appears, dig up and burn.

*Monarda didyma*
BERGAMOT
Creeping perennial with Eau-de-Cologne-scented leaves and scarlet flowers.

*Z 4; H 1m (3ft); S 60cm (24in).*
Grow in sun or part shade in rich,
light moist soil. Sow seed of species
in spring. Plant 45cm (18in) apart.
Divide every 3 years, discarding dead
centres. Take root cuttings in spring,
and stem cuttings in summer.

*Myrica cerifera*
WAX MYRTLE
Evergreen shrub with spicy resinous leaves
and berries covered in balsamic wax.
*Z 6; H 10m (30ft); S 3m (10ft).*
Grow in sun or part shade in well-
drained moist, sandy, acid soil.
Remove weak ground-level growth.
Sow seed in autumn or spring or
take semi-ripe cuttings in summer.

*Myrrhis odorata*
SWEET CICELY
Perennial with fern-like aniseed leaves
and umbels of small white flowers.
*Z 5; H 1.3m (4½ft); S 1m (3ft).*
Plant in light shade in humus-rich
soil. Sow outside in autumn; seed
requires several months of winter
temperatures to germinate. Self-seeds.
Allow 75cm (30in) spacing. Divide
in autumn after plant dies down.

*Myrtus communis*
SWEET MYRTLE
Shrub with small evergreen leaves,
5-petalled ivory flowers and berries,
all with a sweet and spicy scent.
*Z 8; H 5m (15ft); S 3m (10ft).*
Almost frost hardy. In warm areas,
grow in full sun in a sheltered
position in well-drained neutral to
alkaline soil. Protected during the
winter, it may survive temperatures
down to –10°C (14°F), but prefers an
average min temp of 5°C (40°F). Take
stem cuttings in mid- or late-summer.
Transplant to large pots. An ideal tidy
conservatory or topiary plant.

*Narcissus poeticus*
POETS NARCISSUS
Bulb with white or yellow late spring
flowers with intense floral perfume.
*Z 4; H 50cm (18in); S 15cm (6in).*

Plant bulbs one and a half times
deeper than their size in moist well-
drained soil in dappled shade in late
summer or early autumn. Do not cut
leaves until 4–6 weeks after flowering.
Or plant in deep pots. Propagate by
dividing bulbs at the base or by
offsets (small baby bulbs).

*Nepeta cataria*
CATNIP
Camphor-minty herbaceous leaf
and small tubular lavender flower.
*Z 3; H 1m (3ft); S 60cm (24in).*
Sun or light shade in well-drained soil.
Sow seed in spring. Take softwood
cuttings in late spring. Transplant to
30cm (12in). Cut back in autumn.
Plants sown *in situ* are less likely to be
damaged by cats than transplanted
plants, which may need protection.

*Ocimum basilicum*
BASIL
Annuals to short-lived perennials,
offering many leaf sizes and spicy scents.
*Z 10; H 60cm (24in); S 38cm (15in).*
Tender. Warm sun, well-drained
moist soil. Water at midday, not in
the evening. Sow seed thinly with
heat. Avoid over-watering: seedlings
are prone to 'damping off'. Protect
from wind, scorching sun and frost.

*Oenothera biennis*
EVENING PRIMROSE
Biennial or annual with large yellow or
white, sweetly scented evening flowers.
*Z 4; H 1.5m (5ft); S 30cm (12in).*
Sunny, open position in dry soil. Sow
seed in spring to early summer. Self-
seeds in light soil. Transplant to 30cm
(12in) by autumn. May need staking.

*Origanum Majorana,*
*O. onites* and *O. vulgare*
SWEET MARJORAM, POT
MARJORAM & OREGANO
Small leaved perennials with savoury
scent and small white to dark pink
flowers. Sweet Majoram is half hardy
with sweet-spicy-scented soft leaves.
*Z 5; H 1m (3ft); S 75cm (30in).*

Grow in full sun, gold forms prefer
midday shade in well-drained dryish,
nutrient-rich alkaline soil. Sow seed
in spring; germination can be slow.
Divide in spring or autumn. Take root
cuttings late spring to midsummer.
Transplant to 45cm (18in). Cut back
plants by two-thirds before winter or
leave seed heads as bird food.

*Paeonia officinalis*
PEONY
Perennial with indented foliage and
single or double huge, sweetly scented
summer blooms in red, pink or white.
*Z 6; H & S 60cm (24in).*
Grow in sun or part shade in rich,
well-drained soil in a sheltered
position. Dislikes disturbance. Sow
seed, which may take 3 years to
germinate, in autumn. Divide in
autumn or spring; take root cuttings
in winter. Tree Peony can be layered
or semi-ripe cuttings taken in spring.

*Pelargonium capitatum/graveolens/spp*
SCENTED GERANIUMS
Tender perennials with rose-green-
scented leaves and small flowers. Other
varieties offer lemon, peppermint, apple
and spice scents.
*Z 10; H & S 1m (3ft).*
Grow in pots in well-drained
compost. In winter keep in sunny,
warm, well-ventilated indoor space.
Sow in early spring or take 7.5cm
(3in) tip cuttings in late summer or
in spring from over-wintered plants.
Pinch out growing tips when 15cm
(6in). Liquid feed every 10 days
in summer.

*Petroselinum crispum*
PARSLEY
Biennial with curled leaves, umbels of
tiny cream flowers and pungent seed.
*Z 8 (grow as an annual in colder*
*regions); H 80cm (32in); S 30cm (12in).*
Frost hardy. Grow in sun or part
shade in rich, moist, well-drained,
deeply dug neutral to alkaline soil.
Sow seed in succession from spring
to late summer. To speed germination

(which takes 3–7 weeks), soak seed
overnight in warm water and pour
boiling water in the drill before
sowing. Self-seeds freely. Thin to
22cm (9in) and keep watered and
weed-free. Give cloche protection
from winter weather and wildlife.

*Pogostemon cablin*
PATCHOULI
Tender perennial with violet-marked
white flowers and nettle-like leaves
with penetrating earthy-scent.
*Z 11; H & S 1m (3ft).*
Grow in humid heated glasshouse
(min. 17°C [65°F] ) in peaty compost.
Sow in spring; take greenwood
cuttings in late spring; divide in
spring or autumn.

*Polianthes tuberosa*
TUBEROSE
Tuberous perennial with spikes of
exotically perfumed white flowers.
*Z 9; H 50cm (20in); S 20cm (8in).*
Tender. Grow in a warm, sunny
position during the summer, but lift
in autumn and store in sand away
from frost. Under glass, grow singly
in pots in manure-enriched, fibrous
loam. In full growth, water well and
feed fortnightly; dry off as leaves fade
in winter. Propagate by sowing seed
or removing offsets in spring.

*Rosa* species
ROSE
Deciduous shrubs and climbers with
prickly stems and flowers of a variety
of colours and scents.
*Z 2–9; H 25cm-10m (10in–30ft);*
*S 25cm-7m (10in–22ft).*
Grow in an open, sunny or light
position in medium-rich, well-drained
loamy soil. Provide protection from
strong winds, but ensure good air
circulation. Sow ripe seed of species
in autumn or take hardwood cuttings
of all types in autumn. Plant from
autumn to spring; lightly prune in
spring; deadhead in summer. Banana
skins are a good Rose fertilizer: bury
them among the roots.

*Rosmarinus officinalis*
ROSEMARY
Shrub with narrow resinous leaves
and small blue, white or pink flowers.
*Z 6; H & S 2m (6ft).*
Frost hardy. Grow in a sunny
position in well-drained soil. Chalky
soil gives a smaller but more fragrant
plant. Provide protection from cold
winters and biting spring winds.
Rosemary can be grown in a pot,
sunk into the ground in summer
and removed to a greenhouse or
windowsill for the winter.
Germination of seed is erratic,
cuttings of all types are easy.

*Salvia officinalis*
SAGE
Shrub with textured aromatic evergreen
leaves and small mauve-blue flowers.
*Z 5; H 80cm (32in); S 1m (3ft).*
Grow in full sun in light, dry, well-
drained alkaline soil. Grow species
from seed. All forms take easily from
cuttings. Plant 45–60cm (18–24in)
apart. Cut back after flowering;
replace woody plants every 4–5 years.
Prune frequently to keep bushy.
Yellowing leaves can mean roots need
more space. A small green caterpillar
eats the leaves; remove it by hand,
or prune off and burn the leaves.

*Salvia sclarea*
CLARY SAGE
Biennial with large grey leaves and spikes
of dusty-lilac to rose flowers all with
pungent muscatel scent.
*Z 5; H 1m (3ft); S 60cm (24in).*
Sow seed in spring or summer. Self-
seeds in light soils. Dislikes wet winters.

*Santolina* species
SANTOLINA
Evergreen subshrub with silver, finely
cut pungent foliage and yellow flowers.
*Z 7; H 60cm (24in); S 1m (3ft).*
Grow in full sun in well-drained,
preferably sandy soil. If soil is too
rich, the growth will be soft and less
silvery. Take 5–8cm (2–3in) stem
cuttings in spring or from midsummer

to autumn (give protection in frosty
weather). Grow plants 50cm (20in)
apart. Clip to shape in spring or
summer, never in frosty weather.
Deadhead in autumn. If temperatures
drop below –15°C (5°F), give
protection with a sleeve of 2 layers of
chicken wire filled with straw, spruce
or bracken, 13cm (5in) thick.

*Saponaria officinalis*
SOAPWORT
Spreading perennial with soft pink
flowers, wafting a raspberry-sorbet scent.
*Z 4; H & S 60cm (24in).*
Grow in sun or part shade in fertile,
moist soil. Rampant. Sown plants are
variable, so obtain propagating
material from a well-scented mother
plant. Divide the plant or take root
runners from late autumn to early
spring. Grow 60cm (24in) apart. Use
twiggy sticks to support the stems;
cut back after flowering to induce a
second blooming.

*Satureja hortensis* and *S. Montana*
SAVORY
Summer Savory (annual) and Winter
Savory (perennial) have narrow, aromatic
leaves and small pale flowers. Summer
savory has a sweeter flavour.
*Z 8; H 50cm (20in); S 75cm (30in).*
Grow in full sun in well-drained,
chalky, rich soil (moderately fertile for
Winter Savory). Sow seed in spring.
Sow Winter Savory in early autumn
when ripe, press lightly; and do not
cover with soil. Take side cuttings in
summer; divide in spring or autumn.
Allow 45cm (18in) between
perennials, 23cm (9in) between
annuals. Straggly perennials benefit
from hard late-spring pruning. Cut
back annuals in early summer to
prevent plants becoming woody.

*Syringa vulgaris*
LILAC
Deciduous shrub with heart-shaped
leaves and honey-vanilla-scented flowers.
*Z 5; H 7m (22ft); S 5m (15ft).*
Grow in a sunny, open position, but

sheltered from wind, in fertile neutral
to alkaline loam enriched with
manure. Remove faded flowerheads
and suckers from young plants. Prune
old and dead wood after flowering.
Mulch and feed well. Take summer
softwood cuttings or autumn semi-
ripe cuttings and put in a cold frame.
Propagate species from seed or
suckers. Plant 3.5–5m (11–15ft)
apart in spring or autumn.

*Tanacetum balsamita*
ALECOST
Perennial with scalloped, mint-scented
leaves and small daisy flowers.
*Z 6; H 80cm (32in); S 45cm (18in).*
Grow in full sun in rich, well-drained
soil. Divide roots in spring or autumn.
Seed is not viable in cool climates.

*Tanacetum vulgare*
TANSY
Perennial with rosemary-scented,
feathery leaves and acid yellow flowers.
*Z 4; H 1.2m (4ft); S indefinite.*
A vigorous spreader in full sun or
light shade in any soil not too wet.
Sow seed in spring or divide creeping
rootstock in spring or autumn.
Transplant to 60cm (24in).

*Thymus* species
THYME
Subshrubs (woody stems) or creeping
species (rooting stems) with a variety of
leaf colour, flower colour and scent.
*Z 5–7; H 38cm (15in); S 50cm (20in).*
Grow in full sun in light, well-drained,
preferably alkaline soil. Take 5–8cm
(2–3in) 'heeled' stem cuttings any time
except in winter. Divide roots or layer
stems in spring or autumn. Sow species
seed in spring. Transplant to 25cm
(10in). In summer, prune frequently.
In very cold areas, protect in winter.

*Tropaeolum majus*
NASTURTIUM
Climbing or dwarf annual with peppery
leaves, large seeds and orange flowers.
*Z 8; H 2m or 60cm (6 ft or 24in);
S 24cm (9in).*

Full sun or partial shade in free-
draining, moist, average to poor
soil. Poor soil encourages more
flowers. Sow seeds singly 20cm
(8in) apart in late spring.

*Valeriana officinalis*
VALERIAN
Perennial with compound leaves, clusters
of tiny lilac flowers and foxy-scented root.
*Z 7; H 1.2m (4ft); S indefinite.*
Grow in full sun or light shade –
prefers cool roots and warm foliage –
in rich, moist loam. Sow seed in
spring, pressing it into the soil, but
do not cover with soil. Divide roots
in spring or autumn. Plant 60cm
(24in) apart. Harvest the complete
root in the second season in late
autumn. Discard pale fibrous roots,
slice and dry.

*Viola odorata*
SWEET VIOLET
Perennial with violet or white perfumed
flowers and heart-shaped leaves.
*Z 8; H 15cm (6in); S 30cm (12in).*
Grow 10cm (4in) apart in semi-shade,
with early or late sun, in rich, moist
soil. Propagate from runners. Seed
germination is erratic as many early
flowers miss pollination. Divide older
plants immediately after flowering.

*Zingiber officinale*
GINGER
Tropical perennial with erect stems of
compound leaves, perfumed white
flowers and a knobbly rhizome.
*Z 10; H 1.5m (5ft); S indefinite.*
Tender; min temp –1°C (34°F). Buy
a fresh, plump, culinary rhizome in
spring and plant in well-drained,
neutral to alkaline, humus-rich
compost. Maintain high humidity but
do not over-water. A striking
houseplant, it requires 10 months to
produce new Ginger, which can be
dug up when further new shoots
appear. Clean and dry the rhizome,
which will keep fresh for up to 3
months in a cool, dry place; then dry
in small pieces and grind as required.

# Index